T0142589

ON DISPLAY

Outward Appearance and the Christian Woman

ASHLEY E. BOWMAN

WESTBOW
PRESS®
A DIVISION OF THOMAS NELSON
& ZONDERVAN

Scripture quotations are from The Holy Bible, English Standard Version®
(ESV®), copyright © 2001 by Crossway, a publishing ministry of
Good News Publishers. Used by permission. All rights reserved.

WestBow Press books may be ordered through booksellers or by contacting:

WestBow Press
A Division of Thomas Nelson & Zondervan
1663 Liberty Drive
Bloomington, IN 47403
www.westbowpress.com
1 (866) 928-1240

ISBN: 978-1-5127-3359-4 (sc)
ISBN: 978-1-5127-3360-0 (hc)
ISBN: 978-1-5127-3358-7 (e)

Library of Congress Control Number: 2016903729

Print information available on the last page.

WestBow Press rev. date: 04/07/2016

This book is dedicated to the man of
my dreams, Adam Bowman.
Your love, your honesty, and our
marriage have been life-altering—
for me as a woman and, more
importantly, as a child of God.
I am so blessed to be married to you
and to call you my best friend.
Thank you for walking this road called life with me.
I love you.

"Whatever your season of life, God
has called you to beauty:
To a continual growth of internal beauty
by dwelling in him and growing in your
relationship with his Son Jesus.
To a development of the external beauty that
he has blessed you with in order to bring him,
the perfect designer, glory and praise."
-Introduction

CONTENTS

ACKNOWLEDGEMENTS

It seems silly to attempt to name all the people who have been influential in this process. First of all, let any glory gained through this project go the Lord Jesus. Jesus, You are the Perfect Designer, the Creator of mankind, the Divine Artist designing creation and the beauty of mankind. Your love story to us in the Bible has transformed my understanding of life, love, and beauty as a whole and inspired me to make life changes to bring you glory. May this project simply be another way to honor you and your name.

Secondly, thank you to my wonderful husband, Adam, who encouraged and challenged me to put my passion on paper, and who daily sacrificed in order to make this book possible. Now that this project is complete, I will try to be more faithful at baking you goodies and not sending you to work with skimpy lunch boxes in the morning.

I would also like to express sincere thanks to my dear friends Caitlin Gutierrez, Kristin Dewey, Zach and Dina-Rae Scott, Karalie Messer, and Daniel Olewiler for your assistance with and feedback on this project; Grace Cristo for all your title and cover input; Adam Howard at Three-Seven Designs for your excellent cover design; Monica Gee for your amazing editing skills; and Pastor Justin Bleuer, Pastor John Beukema, Dr. Milo Thompson, and my family Justin and Mandy Hoffman and Bonnie Bowman, for your wisdom, assistance, input, and critique as I walked through this process. Thank you for being willing to tell me the truth, to be gracious, and to challenge me according to the Word.

FOREWORD

We gathered around the floor of a dimly lit apartment, forty giggling college girls. We sat on colorful couch pillows and talked in excited whispers. It wasn't very often that a man ventured onto the grounds of the all-girl apartment complex of The Master's College. But we weren't just waiting for any man. Our special guest that night was Charles W. Smith, our beloved Bible professor who had devoted fifty years of his life to Christian education and would very soon be with the Lord. Later, I would spend the last two years of my college career living in a dorm named after him.

I don't remember much of what he said to us that night almost fifteen years ago. I know he talked about marriage, singleness, and biblical womanhood. I remember the reverent hush that lingered in the room as we stared at a man who radiated the beauty of Christ while wearing a body dying of cancer. But one thing he said will always stick with me. A timid student asked, "If we are supposed to be discreet and meek, how can we get guys to notice us?" The professor's eyes twinkled and he said, "The mousetrap doesn't chase the mouse . . . but it does put out pretty good bait." In a room full of women who had been taught that beauty is primarily internal, this came as a shock. His statement challenged our thinking. We looked at each other. "You mean . . . it's okay to focus on the outside, too?"

Christian women face a challenge. With society pushing us to be consumed with the outside and churches telling us to pursue beauty on the inside, where can we strike a balance—if there even is one? Where does biblical beauty lie? Is it exclusively internal? Should we devote time and energy to the external as well? If so, how much? Where do we draw the line between stewardship and vanity?

In this treasure of a book, the author takes a look at beauty from a refreshingly unique perspective. Ashley gets personal and practical while remaining theologically grounded—and she's not afraid to raise a few eyebrows. For the last several years Ashley has been on a mission to help Christian women think rightly about beauty—not just for themselves, but also for their husbands and their families.

Ashley's purpose in writing pivots around the gospel. Every part of this book points us back to beauty in its truest form: God's plan of salvation.

This book is for a young single woman wondering how to prepare for a spouse. It's for a newlywed eager to be a good wife. It's for a woman married for many years who wants to rekindle the flame.

So get ready to have your view of biblical beauty challenged. Prepare for a fresh start fueled by the hope and encouragement of the gospel.

Sara Wallace,
Author of *The Gospel-Centered Mom*

INTRODUCTION

I will never forget my first blog post about external beauty. I had been feeling pretty convinced of the necessity for women to show love for their spouses by caring for their outer bodies. After some thought and conversation with Adam, I attempted to communicate something to that effect rather generically on my personal blog. It wasn't long before I had a few responses from women who obviously thought very differently than I did and who demonstrated that in their lifestyles and in their responses to me. I understood right away that while this was an uncomfortable topic for any woman to discuss, for Christian women in particular it was somehow more of a taboo subject. One in which women were even less willing to hear from a woman who loved to run and exercise.

After all, there are so many reasons that I would seem disqualified to talk. I'm an avid runner and lifter. It comes easy for me, right? Honestly, no. Just recently I found myself laughing when someone described me as having a "natural runner's form". Really? I think not. Little do these women know how much I have worked to change my understanding of my responsibilites as a woman and, later, as a wife. An understanding that would bring about significant change in me: from an absolute abhorrence of activities such as working out, running, and lifting, to having a passion that will soon find its outlet in having a certification as a personal trainer. What changed, you ask? I hope to share with you in the upcoming chapters the passion and the heart change that took place.

Before I start though, I would ask that you read this one statistic: currently, 80 percent of women in the U.S. are dissatisfied with their appearance.[1] Unless you're in that 20 percent, you already feel inadequate, unattractive, fat, out of shape, and not as pretty as the girl next door. My heart in this book is not to worsen that already sickening feeling. My desire in writing this is to take those desires for beauty that we all have and to encourage you that God is the author of beauty. He has called us to use our bodies for his glory. I'm not advocating for a specific workout schedule, dress size, or number on a scale. I simply hope to show you that health is possible, even biblical, for the Christian woman. Your body matters to God.

Beauty. While there are a variety of opinions as to what is fashionable, attractive, and beautiful today, as a whole, society's focus on external and physical beauty has grown exponentially. Even television shows are dedicated solely to the topic. There are complete, multi-season reality shows about models, fashion, and on what is and is not socially acceptable to wear. There are regional, national, and televised competitions that focus simply on the external beauty that both men and women have (or have not) been blessed with. The prettiest of entire regions, states, nations, and the world have been critiqued, labeled, and rewarded—all in an attempt to find and define what is the most beautiful. Commercials offer us products to help us meet a specific standard of beauty. Procedures have been created to help the older generations re-gain their youthful beauty. People, young and old, have elected to undergo life-altering surgeries to change their

---

[1] http://psychcentral.com/blog/archives/2012/06/02/why-do-women-hate-their-bodies/

personal appearances, to enhance or reduce body parts—to edit perceived "flaws"—all in the name of external beauty.

Within this intense cultural focus on the external, Christians have taken the extreme opposite view: exclusively emphasizing character development and what we have termed "inner beauty." Amidst the desire to refocus the fleshly heart on eternal things, we have taken the physical body and disregarded its role and ability to glorify God. In reality, we can glorify God even with something as temporary as external beauty and physical health. In fact, biblically, we find a balance to our extremes of obsession with or rejection of external care. After detailed study, I believe God's intention for the external offers a clear eternal focus, providing us with a spiritual motive for caring for our temporal bodies. Resulting in giving your best to something that has long been viewed as secular.

Whether married or single, the Christian woman of the 21st century finds herself torn between the desire to be externally beautiful and the priority to develop an internal spiritual beauty. However, sin has found its way into our lives and the Church has responded unbiblically to the world's obsession with the external. Her understanding has been twisted until she now thinks that these two kinds of beauty are mutually exclusive. Christian women are left focusing on "developing" internal beauty and warned against giving attention to the external because it is viewed as shortsighted, temporal, and less than spiritual.

However, internal beauty and external beauty are hardly related. Their only similarity is that they were both designed by an holy God for the purpose of bringing him glory. In singleness, the external should be used to glorify God through the care given to modesty, health, honoring Christ as the groom, and protecting the heart and mind of any future spouse God might bring into her life. Careful dedication to the external beauty of a married woman is also God glorifying. A woman is called to give her best to God by the way she lives and what she does with her health.

She is also called to honor her husband, demonstrate her love, and fulfill her marriage vows by offering to him an external beauty that assists him in his walk with the Lord, encourages him to walk in purity, and supports him in his God-created design.

Whatever your season of life, God has called you to beauty: to a continual growth of internal beauty by dwelling in him and growing in your relationship with his Son Jesus. To a development of the external beauty that he has blessed you with in order bring him, the perfect designer, glory and praise.

PART I

INTERNAL BEAUTY

CHAPTER 1

What the Scripture Says

The Bible has much to say about the heart of mankind. Scripture declares the insides of mankind as "deceitful above all things, and desperately sick"[2], sinful in our very nature—from birth and before birth, conceived from sinful beings into sin[3]—, children of God's holy wrath[4], foolish at heart[5], and full of evil intent at the core[6]. That is quite the list full of characteristics. Unfortunately, those characteristics are anything but beautiful. With those descriptions in mind, it seems frivolous to discuss anything in regards to innate internal beauty within women. It is pointless to discuss anything other than the nasty, rotten smell of death that we can see within the unredeemed heart of mankind.

Of course, man was created "good", beautiful, and perfect by the hand of God the Creator. Yet, sin, through the deception of the devil, was introduced quickly, and what was once beautiful as it was originally designed became damaged. What was once a source of pleasure to a holy God was now disdainful. While his

---

[2]   Jeremiah 17:9

[3]   Psalm 51:5

[4]   Ephesians 2:3

[5]   Proverbs 22:15

[6]   Genesis 8:21

original creation had been perfectly designed, sin, like leprosy, spread until it had not only affected the internal soul of man but also the exterior appearance and all the interactions that this once-beautiful creation enjoyed. Everything intended for this creation has been and continues to be tainted by the disease of sin. Wherein lies the internal beauty?

When Christ Jesus offered himself on Calvary, he took upon himself the disdain of the creator for this fallen creature. Suddenly, the holy Son was the One on whom God the Father could not turn his eyes. His perfection traded for our sin-blackened hearts, as he became our sin, so that we might gain his righteousness[7]. Of course, only those who have recognized their own disease-ridden hearts and accepted the perfect sacrifice Christ offered on their behalf have been healed of the ever-consuming, rancid disease called sin, and therein lies the beauty. Internal beauty is then the forgiveness of sin and the radical transformation of a soul bound by death and separated from the holy creator into a soul that is reconciled to the Father and finally able to please God and bring to him the glory due his name.

Unfortunately, it is this understanding of real beauty that is quickly lost among Christians as we become comfortable in our new skin. Suddenly, we lose sight of who we were and the true beauty of Christ's sacrifice is lost upon us, replaced by an ideology that says internal beauty is something that can be attained on our own accord. How prideful we are! The only thing beautiful about the Christian heart is the work of the transforming power of Jesus Christ; any work of our own is "like a polluted garment"[8].

Remember to think on what we all know so well, the biblical account of Christ, with a renewed passion as we begin this discussion of external beauty. Now that we are reminded of the truth about internal beauty as result of Christ's work in

---

[7]   2 Corinthians 5:21
[8]   Isaiah 64:6

our hearts, we need to reexamine some of the verses that have frequently been placed before women in order to challenge us to pursue internal beauty.

Even before Paul addressed the issue of women having braided hair and costly jewelry, Christ Jesus himself addressed the pharisees of his day on this same subject. Matthew 23 is a clear record of the heart of Jesus regarding the state of internal beauty. Addressing hypocrisy amongst the spiritual leaders of the day, Jesus said, in verse 27, "Woe to you, scribes and Pharisees, hypocrites! For you are like whitewashed tombs, which outwardly appear beautiful, but within are full of dead people's bones and all uncleanness."[9] This is a well-known passage among Christians on the topic of hypocrisy, but I challenge you to take a closer look at this in light of the discussion of beauty.

Here we have men, spiritual leaders of the Jewish society, calling others to a high level of spirituality. They were, however, still unregenerate and full of sin internally. They were professing the "beauty" of spirituality while covering their own rotting, sinful flesh with pretty garments. Like skeletons donned in tuxedos, these spiritually dead men were called out by the One who knew their hearts. Their spiritual beauty was only superficial. Thus, Christ challenges the ideology that internal beauty (for men and women alike) is anything that can be attained on one's own. It is not found in performing spiritual exercises, applying spiritual makeup, speaking spiritual words, or conducting spiritual rituals. Otherwise, the pharisees would have found the key. Instead, Jesus challenges them, and us, that true internal beauty is found in the transformed, spiritually revived heart.

Defining internal beauty as a heart made new by the truth and love of Christ and his saving work on the cross provides us with a clearer understanding of Peter's discussion of beauty in 1 Peter 3. "Do not let your adorning be external—the braiding of hair

---

[9]   Matthew 23:27

and the putting on of gold jewelry, or the clothing you wear—but let your adorning be the hidden person of the heart with the imperishable beauty of a gentle and quiet spirit, which in God's sight is very precious. For this is how the holy women who hoped in God used to adorn themselves . . . "[10] The issue of beauty here that is so often addressed is the braiding of hair and the wearing of gold jewelry or fancy clothing, but the heart of what Peter was addressing was the temptation of whitewashed tombs. In fact, I think it foolish to believe that Peter was not acknowledging the temptation, as women do, to focus too much on the external. To emphasize the presentation so much that we find ourselves possessing all the appearance of holiness and spiritual beauty but forget that the true woman of God finds her beauty internally in the regenerating work of Christ. The external, while important, is a distracting and pointless aim at attaining beauty if the inside is rotting away in sin.

The Proverbs wisely state: "Charm is deceitful, and beauty is vain, but a woman who fears the LORD is to be praised."[11] Interestingly enough, this verse is often used to warn the godly man against seeking simply physical beauty when looking for a spouse, but the instruction is just as much for the godly woman. The source of your beauty, women, is in the fear of the Lord. Once again, the Scripture reminds us that internal beauty is not an act of the will or an external demonstration, but is found in losing oneself in the fear of a holy God.

Second Corinthians 5:17–21 reminds the believer to hide oneself away in the covering of the righteousness of Christ. Colossians 3 addresses the issue of putting off the old self and donning the new character of Christ and specifically, in verse 3, reminds the child of God that she has died and her life is hidden away with Christ. Therefore, in addressing beauty and

---

[10]   1 Peter 3:3–5
[11]   Proverbs 31:30

the often-encouraged focus to be beautiful on the inside, let me challenge you in the full counsel of Scripture. Attaining beauty in the interior is merely hiding oneself away in Christ, in his righteousness, putting "to death therefore what is earthly in you. . . put on then, as God's chosen ones, holy and beloved,"[12] the character of Christ.

---

[12]   Colossians 3:5, 12

CHAPTER 2

What the Church Has Done

As we come to understand what real internal beauty is and how it is attained biblically, we begin to understand more and more the heart behind the Apostle Paul's exhortation to Christian women to focus on internal growth. So often, as women, we find it easy to focus on appearance, whether physical or spiritual, and in doing so, neglect the necessity to dwell in Christ. The more women can find our identity in attaching ourselves to the vine, that is Jesus, the more his beauty can shine forth through us, the branches.[13] Therefore, internal beauty is simply found in resting: resting in the work that Christ has already accomplished on our behalf and allowing *his* beauty and perfection to shine through us.

I think we can all agree on this so far. This concept is nothing radical. We can understand the deception of our own hearts, the ugliness of the internal sin into which we are born, and the necessity of Christ to remove our hearts of stone and replace them with beautiful hearts of flesh.[14] However, this is where I begin to step on toes and challenge classical thinking. As a general statement, Christians have allowed the challenge of Peter

---

[13] John 15:5
[14] Ezekiel 36:26

and Timothy in calling us to focus on internal beauty and the indwelling of Christ to be an excuse to forget that the external is important or at least to misrepresent the heart of Christ in this matter.

While you might say that is an overly broad statement, a 2006 Purdue study found that the fundamental (specifically Baptist) Christian churches lead the world in obesity, claiming 30 percent of those diagnosed with obesity. Those in other religions like Buddhism and Judaism claim only 1 percent. In fact, Christian churches have actually been called a "feeding ground" for the problem of obesity.[15] This is not a personal opinion. This is not my opinion based on the number of churches I have attended or the number of people I know who could shed a few pounds. A national study found that Christians as a whole have seemingly thrown out any focus on the external in an attempt to focus solely on the internal.

Unfortunately, we have misrepresented the heart of Christ in this matter. While I'm not here to address obesity as a main topic, in order to proceed with the understanding of our responsibility as women to take care of our external bodies, we must understand the heart of God in regards to this issue of external appearance. We must see that it is a responsibility that all women, married and single, have before both God and man. If we look at the full counsel of Scripture and the topic of outward appearance, we need to address a well-known passage that discusses a godly woman. Proverbs 31, the go-to passage for a woman who seeks to be godly, addresses external appearance in verses 17, 21, and 22: "She dresses herself with strength and makes her arms strong . . . She is not afraid of snow for her household, for all her household

---

[15] http://www.churchleaders.com/pastors/pastor-articles/161342-doctor-calls-churches-a-feeding-ground-for-obesity.html; http://www.foxnews.com/opinion/2012/06/03/obesity-epidemic-in-america-churches/

are clothed in scarlet. She makes bed coverings for herself; her clothing is fine linen and purple."

Even just a quick overview of these three verses allows us to see a few key things about the woman of God. In verse 17, she makes a choice to walk in strength and make herself strong. "She dresses" and "makes her arms strong"—these are actions of choice. This speaks directly to her focus on her own physical abilities. She makes it a point to develop a physical strength in her body. In verse 21, she clothes her household in fine garments. Exodus 39 tells us that the colors of the priestly garment included scarlet, indigo, and purple[16]; it is significant then that the woman of God discussed in Proverbs 31 is dressed in both red (vs. 21) and purple (v. 22). She wears fine linen—something we know was handmade and required hours of hard labor to weave—so already we can understand that the woman of God puts time and hard work into how she and her household look on the outside. This is not a passing thought of hers. In fact, the external appearance of herself and those in her care is something to which she has devoted hours of time and serious physical labor in order to attain.

Sarah, Rebecca, Rachel, and Esther are all women in the Bible whose physical beauty was mentioned. Each of one their beautiful appearances were utilized by God in the greater plan of salvation. For example, Rachel was the chosen bride for Jacob, yet her father forced Jacob to also marry his older daughter, Leah. Rachel was known as being "beautiful in form and appearance" while Leah's "eyes were weak".[17] Rachel went on to be the mother of Joseph, and the sons of both women eventually became the twelve tribes of Israel. Esther's physical beauty is what God used to place her in the position as wife to King Ahasuerus during a volatile time for the people of Israel. Esther 2:7–17 tells us that of all the young virgins of Israel, Esther had a beautiful figure and was lovely to

---

[16] http://www.studylight.org/dic/hbd/view.cgi?number=T1332
[17] Genesis 29:17

look upon, and because of that, caught the eye of the king. She was added to his harem and later became queen. As a result of her position, she played an influential role in God's preservation of the chosen people of Israel.

As demonstrated through these Old Testament narratives, the external beauty of a woman is not pointless and futile. God uses even what is temporary—the fleeting beauty of a woman—-to accomplish his eternal plan. Instead of recognizing this, evangelical Christians have deemed a lack of interest in the external as more holy than a concern with exterior appearances. I myself have been confronted with comments about my out-of-place priorities, met resistance at my research of this topic, and faced skepticism that a topic about something as temporary as external beauty and the responsibility women have before God could have biblical backing.

Young girls have been warned against giving too much attention to their appearance. Parents have been cautioned about praising physical appearance too frequently, having been counseled to "make sure [their] comments related to appearance, weight, and body shape of [their] daughter (and others) are scarce,"[18] as if any encouragement in the external devalues the internal, while, in reality, they work hand-in-hand with each other.

Matthew 6:16–18 warns against the mentality that says neglecting one's external appearance in order to appear holy is God-honoring: "And when you fast, do not look gloomy like the hypocrites, for they disfigure their faces that their fasting may be seen by others. Truly, I say to you, they have received their reward. But when you fast, anoint your head and wash your face, that your fasting may not be seen by others but by your Father who is in secret. And your Father who sees in secret will reward you."

---

[18] http://www.focusonthefamily.com/parenting/sexuality preventing_the_sexualization_of_your_daughter/talking_to_your_daughter.aspx

Jesus calls his followers to not draw attention to themselves by avoiding taking care of their outward appearance in an attempt to seem more spiritual than others. He challenges them to understand that the heart of man is seen by the Father "in secret" and that one's appearance does not directly equate with the status of one's internal beauty. Therefore, we can see that Jesus warns his followers against both extremes: focusing solely on the external, which avoids the internal problem of sin found in the heart of mankind, and on the other hand neglecting the external completely. The balance, instead, is found in a serious focus on the internal beauty found in dwelling in Christ, as well as a focused, necessary care to external things.

PART II

SIN AND ITS EFFECT ON BEAUTY

CHAPTER 3

Women + Sin

Sin—its wretched effect on our lives started before we were born. Our hearts are at their formation, sinful by nature. Its effect flourishes as we grow up in a fallen world and find ourselves influenced by the surrounding society and enticed by all that appeals to the desires of the flesh, the desires of the eyes, and the pride of life[19]. As it has so intimately affected every area of humanity, so have all women experienced the ways in which sin has an increasingly massive influence on the understanding that they have of beauty.

It is important in any discussion of this topic, to first address the myriad of pressures, unrealistic expectations, and temptations that women are facing in this sex-crazed world. Even more importantly to address these pressures in a book that seeks to challenge Christian women to do something radical and focus more (radical, indeed!) on the external in order to fulfill their God-intended purpose. In fact, when I first shared the concept of this book with some dear friends and family, the initial response was concern over not adding to the already overwhelming pressure that women are facing today. I agree; these pressures

---

[19]   1 John 2:16

need to be addressed. However, it is important to engage these struggles, perceptions, and temptations in light of the Scripture and what Christ has called us to.

Unrealistic Pressures/Expectations

The world of technology is a wonderful thing. Technology has been used to advance great discoveries to help society, to advance medicine, to manage big business, and to spread the word globally on everything from world news to fashion. Technology has changed the world in more ways than we realize. The computer has changed the simple task of letter writing to include emails, chats, private messages and open forums on a variety of social networks. In the same way, the introduction of technology into the world of fashion has played an enormous role in the misconception of beauty and physical expectations. It has added an intense pressure for women to reach a specific standard of external beauty. In fact, publications such as Glamour,[20] IdealBite,[21] The Huffington Post,[22] Beauty Redefined,[23] and the New York Times[24] all host articles discussing the reality of photoshopped pictures of models, ad campaigns, commercials, and even news anchors—and the effect it is having on the expectations that women have for themselves.

---

[20] http://www.glamour.com/health-fitness/2012/02/retouching-how-much-is-too-much

[21] http://idealbite.com/100-percent-of-what-you-see-in-fashion-magazines-is-retouched/

[22] http://www.huffingtonpost.com/2010/03/29/majority-of-beauty-ads-di_n_517276.html

[23] http://www.beautyredefined.net/photoshopping-altering-images-and-our-minds/

[24] http://www.nytimes.com/2009/05/28/fashion/28RETOUCH.html?pagewanted=all&_r=0

Thankfully, photoshopping models and celebrities in order to make them more sexually appealing or to convince the consumer to buy a specific product has become understood as a real danger to women. It has given them unrealistic physical expectations of themselves. In fact, this has resulted in the American Medical Association (AMA) adopting a new policy in June 2011, wherein they "encourage advertising associations to work with public and private sector organizations concerned with child and adolescent health to develop guidelines for advertisements, especially those appearing in teen-oriented publications, that would discourage the altering of photographs in a manner that could promote unrealistic expectations of appropriate body image."[25] AMA board member Barbara L. McAneny, MD, later said in a press release: "The appearance of advertisements with extremely altered models can create unrealistic expectations of appropriate body image. In one image, a model's waist was slimmed so severely, her head appeared to be wider than her waist. We must stop exposing impressionable children and teenagers to advertisements portraying models with body types only attainable with the help of photo editing software.'"[26]

It really cannot be said much clearer than Dr. McAneny stated. Because of the use of Photoshop and the alteration of women's bodies in pictures and movies, both young and old, are overwhelmed by the pressure to attain the perfect look. In reality it is nothing more than a farce, a swipe of a keyboard mouse here and there, the digital combination of a variety of "ideal" body parts, and the use of breast augmentations, Botox, butt cushions, synthetic eyelashes, and heavy makeup in order to change reality to fantasy.

The lack of understanding for women facing these unattainable standards compounded with the expectation of the modern man

---

[25]   https://www.govtrack.us/congress/bills/113/hr4341/text

[26]   http://www.medpagetoday.com/MeetingCoverage/AMA/27199

(see Chapter Four) to find a woman with the "sexiest" body feed on each other until we are faced with the current scene of tissue-eating[27] models, surgery-obsessed women, and eating disorders that give us the following statistics.

Media, Perception, Dieting:

- 95% of all dieters will regain their lost weight within 5 years.
- 35% of "normal dieters" progress to pathological dieting. Of those, 20–25% progress to partial or full-syndrome eating disorders.
- The body type portrayed as the ideal in advertising is possessed naturally by only 5% of American females.
- 47% of girls in 5th–12th grade reported wanting to lose weight because of magazine pictures.
- 69% of girls in 5th–12th grade reported that magazine pictures influenced their idea of a perfect body shape.
- 42% of 1st–3rd grade girls want to be thinner.
- 81% of 10 year olds are afraid of being fat.

Mortality Rates:

Although eating disorders have the highest mortality rate of any mental disorder, the mortality rates reported on those who suffer from eating disorders can vary considerably between studies and sources. Part of the reason why there is a large variance in the reported number of deaths caused by eating disorders is because those who suffer from an eating disorder may ultimately die of heart failure, organ failure, malnutrition or suicide. Often, the medical complications of death are reported instead of the eating disorder that compromised a person's health.

---

[27] http://www.huffingtonpost.ca/2013/04/03/vogue-factor_n_3006521.html

According to a study done by colleagues at the American Journal of Psychiatry (2009), crude mortality rates were:

- 4% for anorexia nervosa
- 3.9% for bulimia nervosa
- 5.2% for eating disorder not otherwise specified[28]

Temptations

Knowing these facts can shed quite a light on the expectations a woman places on herself. Knowing the truth can bring comfort to the insecure female with a real, "imperfect" body with skin blemishes, small breasts, a flat booty, and thick thighs. However, it takes more than a mental realization of these to affect real change in our understanding of beauty while society continues to rub an unattainable image in the face of women.

Without a correct view of God's perfect character and design, his masterful creation, his good character, and his immaculate standard, women cannot effectively combat the temptations they face daily. The Bible is full of passages that address these traits of God. It teaches us God's view of his creation and help us combat the temptations of anorexia, bulimia, orthorexia, anorexia athetica, binge eating, surgical implants, physical modification surgery, and even the seemingly less drastic temptations to have to dress perfectly, buy name brand clothes, or wear heavy makeup. The following verses teach us about God and his perfect design for humanity:

- Psalm 139:14 "I praise you, for I am fearfully and wonderfully made. Wonderful are your works; my soul knows it very well."

---

[28] http://www.anad.org/get-information/about-eating-disorders/eating-disorders-statistics/

- Psalm 107:17–20 "Some were fools through their sinful ways, and because of their iniquities suffered affliction; they loathed any kind of food, and they drew near to the gates of death. Then they cried to the LORD in their trouble, and he delivered them from their distress. He sent out his word and healed them, and delivered them from their destruction.."

- Genesis 1:26–28a, 31 "Then God said, 'Let us make man in our image, after our likeness. And let them have dominion over the fish of the sea and over the birds of the heavens and over the livestock and over all the earth and over every creeping thing that creeps on the earth.' So God created man in his own image, in the image of God he created him; male and female he created them. And God blessed them . . . And God saw everything that he had made, and behold, it was very good."

- 1 Corinthians 6:19–20 "Or do you not know that your body is a temple of the Holy Spirit within you, whom you have from God? You are not your own, for you were bought with a price. So glorify God in your body."

- Isaiah 49:16 "Behold, I have engraved you on the palms of my hands; your walls are continually before me."

- Jeremiah 29:11 "For I know the plans I have for you, declares the LORD, plans for welfare and not for evil, to give you a future and a hope."

Of course, this list is not exhaustive; however, these are some of the most pointed passages in discussing God's view of his creation, mankind.

Without Excuse

While some Christian women struggle to fight the unattainable, doctored image by seeking to emulate it, other Christian women have taken the more "spiritual" response by simply not caring. I will never forget my first blog post about external beauty. At that point in my blogging "career" (I use the word lightly), I hardly ever received comments or responses. However on this post, it was only a matter of hours before I had two Christian women pretty vehemently attacking my post for its focus on the "external" and the "temporal." While their intentions were good, their understanding of internal beauty was skewed. Their response to the modern, unattainable body that society is tempting women with had simply been to avoid anything that resembled this deception and simply to focus on what is internal.

While I had a lot of thoughts at that time, their comments to me influenced my desire to write this book, to clarify that focusing on the internal does not excuse an obligation that women have to take care of our external bodies. I would dare to even disagree with those women and say that there is an *eternal* responsibility that we have as women to develop our *external* beauty. Yes, I know. I just made the claim that something that has been viewed by Christian women all over the world as frivolous and unspiritual does, in fact, have spiritual merit. Call me heretical if you wish, but I beg you to continue to read on as I explain to you why this is something I believe. Because of that eternal responsibility, I believe that Christian women are without excuse and should give attention and care to our external bodies.

CHAPTER 4

Men + Sin

It is important that we take the time to address another influence that sin has had on beauty and our understanding of external appearance. As we have just discussed, women throughout the world have a misconstrued understanding of beauty. Through further research, we can see that women's understanding of beauty is not the only view affected. The mindset of men in the world has also been influenced. Sin has damaged the way that men view beauty in women.

Unrealistic Expectations/Misconceptions

Just as we took the time to look at the dangers of photoshopped and medically or otherwise altered models, we need to revisit issue of unrealistic expectations. I hope and pray that women are becoming more and more knowledgeable about how much modern media has tainted the reality of natural beauty, and I seek to assist women in growing in this understanding. But it would be foolish to think that all men already understand this concept or are growing more knowledgeable on this topic. Consider that most men do not understand how women's emotions work, nor understand specifically just how different women are than men. In most cases, they know even less about how women's bodies work.

With this understanding, coupled with what we have recently discussed about media's unreachable standards for women's bodies, let us acknowledge that the men in our lives are seeing the same pictures, watching the same movies, and being offered the same misconstrued version of reality. While women are faced with the pressures to match those unattainable body measurements and proportions for ourselves, our men are being taught to expect what is not realistic. As a result, it is possible—no, probable—for there to be expectations held by the men in our lives to which you may never measure up.

Stop right there. If you're anything like me, that statement of "never measuring up" raises the hairs on the back of your neck. There is nothing more frustrating than trying hard and still not measuring up. I ask that you do not fault the whole male species for this hard-to-hear fact. I myself find this truth hard to swallow. I attribute the fault to the deception of modern media and to the lack of fathers discussing reality with their sons, helping them gain a proper perspective—a topic for another day indeed. This lack of understanding, as we have probably already sensed within ourselves, adds tension to an already sensitive issue. In turn, that tension only puts more pressure on women to attain a body that is "perfect," even if that means it is half-modified with surgeries, implants, syringes, covered in makeup, push-ups and pads, and weighing no more than [insert ideal number here] pounds.

If we set aside our emotions for a moment, we see this rather sad picture: a young man is offered a prize he can never attain because it does not exist. In fact, I begin to see that the problem here is not that my husband desires me to be attractive but that he's been told certain proportions are possible, healthy, natural, and attainable by any woman.

Temptations

Because of the false advertising that this world has directed at men, their temptations are unique. While women are tempted to avoid eating or gaining weight or surgically correct attributes we view as flaws, men are faced with the temptation to seek out and expect the unattainable. As a single person, the temptation would be to find the girl with the most-perfect body or to make harsh, naive judgments on a woman's ability to attain that "beauty" (altered reality) they see in the media. As a married person, the temptation for a husband would be to have and show little appreciation for the work his wife puts in to making herself beautiful and/or to seek to find that unattainable beauty through some other source.

Without Excuse

Before you jump to any conclusions, I am not allowing for the making of excuses in this matter. Let me assure you that, just as women are without excuse for how we have forgotten our eternal responsibility to take care to the external, men also have no excuse with how they handle the temptations they face. Without an eternal perspective, a single young man can find himself judgmental, inconsiderate, temporally focused, and even convinced that he deserves something greater than he does. A single man whose sole focus is the external attributes of a woman is lacking more than the understanding of the unattainable image displayed by society's modern media. He is lacking wisdom and an eternal perspective that reaches beyond the external. Without an eternal perspective in view, a married man can easily find himself caught up in temptations to find justification for a lack of intimacy with his spouse, a disregard for the necessary love and care for his wife, and a justification for a lack of faithfulness in marriage. A married man who lacks love and affection for his wife because she does not match a standard of his in the area of external beauty is also missing the far more important virtue of his purpose as a husband as a reflection of the love that Christ has for the Church.[29] The Church, the body of Christ, is far from perfect. Yet Jesus Christ still offered himself for her and lives to intercede for her even today.[30]

I am in no way justifying any lack of care and gentleness given to women in this area, nor am I justifying a lack of verbally expressed love for wives, insensitivity by husbands, a lack of faithfulness in marriage, pornography, affairs, the pursuit of prostitutes, any emotional, verbal, and/or physical abuse, or any other unrealistic expectations or lack of an eternal perspective as demonstrated by men towards women. However, I am seeking to offer women a different perspective on the false understanding men have been given on beauty and to remind us that their misconceptions are opportunities for some great communication and are in no way a justification for *our* lack of fulfilling our personal, God-given responsibilities. Sin *has* affected both men and women, but the lack of either side to correctly combat temptations and misconceptions by no means justifies the other person's lack of obedience before God.

---

[29]   Ephesians 5:25
[30]   Hebrews 7:25

PART III

THE IMPORTANCE OF
EXTERNAL BEAUTY

CHAPTER 5

Women and God
Understanding the Philosophy

As the Creature

I have already introduced the topic of women and their responsibility before God to care for the external. It's time for us to delve into this topic more directly, that we might see the biblical basis for these claims. It is necessary that we start at the beginning, all the way back in Genesis, with the creation of humankind. It is important to recall the words of the verse that details our creation. Genesis 1:26 reads: "Then God said, 'Let us make man in our image, after our likeness.'" From this first mention of mankind, we see a divine intention. God created mankind to be a physical representation of his own image.

While this verse records the specific creation of the first man and woman, additional Scripture verses remind us that God's intricate role as the creator, sustainer, and designer of life was not limited to the creation of the first two humans but continues to be present in every individual life. In a beautiful hymn of adoration to the creator, King David records the following words: "For you formed my inward parts; you knitted me together in my mother's   womb. I praise you, for I am fearfully and wonderfully made. Wonderful are your works; my soul knows it very well. My frame was not hidden from you, when I was being made in secret, intricately woven in the depths of the earth. Your eyes saw my unformed substance; in your book were written, every one of them, the days that were formed for me, when as yet there was none of them."[31]

There is no man or woman born with whom God is not intimately involved in every step of his or her development. There is no life for whom God does not have a divine purpose that finds its roots back in Genesis 1:26. There is no other purpose for any member of mankind than what is described in the first verse about the creation of Adam and Eve: to demonstrate "[his] likeness." This, of course, is not where this understanding of mankind's purpose ends. With that understanding of a very general purpose, we must learn what that looks like specifically.

Through further reading and studying of the Scripture, we are able to more deeply grasp the purpose of mankind through the following passages:

1 Peter 2:9 says, "But you are a chosen race, a royal priesthood, a holy nation, a people for his own possession, that you may proclaim the excellencies of him who called you out of darkness into his marvelous light."

Ephesians 2:10 reads, "For we are his workmanship, created in Christ Jesus for good works, which God prepared beforehand, that we should walk in them."

John 15:16 says, "You did not choose me, but I chose you and appointed you that you should go and bear fruit and that your fruit should abide . . ."

These verses challenge the believer in Jesus Christ that humans were created and then saved for a specific purpose. It was not a frivolous decision made by God to form a life in the

---

[31]   Psalm 139:13–16

womb, nor to save the soul of his child from eternal damnation. He has saved us for a particular cause, to act as his likeness in this world, to proclaim his excellencies, to walk in the good works he has preplanned for us, and to go and bear fruit for the kingdom of heaven.

Furthermore, 1 Corinthians 10:31 goes on to challenge us that our responsibility to represent Christ in this world does not fall short of influencing every aspect of our lives: "So, whether you eat or drink, or whatever you do, do all to the glory of God." First Corinthians 6:19–20 goes as far as to challenge Christian believers that there are, in fact, eternal ramifications to what is temporal—your body—in the same way that there are consequences for actions taken in other areas of obedience to Christ. There are also repercussions for disregarding what has long been viewed as merely temporal and not worthy of being utilized to glorify God: "Or do you not know that your body is a temple of the Holy Spirit within you, whom you have from God? You are not your own, for you were bought with a price. So glorify God in your body."

Therefore, with the understanding that we are to be representing Christ in everything we do, married with the biblical challenge that there are consequences for what we do with our bodies, the temple of God, need I ask you to think carefully about whether external appearance is important before the Lord? He is the creator, he is the ultimate designer, and he has left no area of our life without purpose in glorifying him. Therefore, "glorify God in your body."

We are really left without excuse, as we read through these passages. We are called to glorify God with our bodies and to do everything—even eating and drinking—in a manner that proclaims his excellence. Once again, there is no excuse for a lack of careful attention to what each of us does with our body: how we feed it, how we dress it, and how we take care of it on a daily basis.

As the Masterpiece

If these verses have not challenged you enough to bring about a change in your perspective on your body and its eternal purpose, let me explain to you a little about God's design for women specifically. In reading through the creation account in Genesis 2, recall the order of creation. At this point in history, the universe has existed for a total of six days. God has created light, darkness, day and night, land and plants, oceans and animals, skies, and every living creature. Then, he designs mankind after his own image. He creates a man from the dirt and calls him "Adam". As the day progresses, he creates again, a woman, to meet the needs of his newest creation.

John MacArthur, in his book *Twelve Extraordinary Women of the Bible*, describes the creation of woman as follows: "Eve, the only being ever directly created by God by the living tissue of another creature, was indeed a singular marvel. God had composed a vast universe of wonders out of nothing. Then he made Adam from a handful of dust. But nothing in the whole expanse of the universe was more wonderful than this woman made from a handful of Adam. If the man represented the supreme species (a race of creatures made in the image of God), Eve was the living embodiment of humanity's glory (1 Cor. 11:7). God had truly saved the best for last. Nothing else would have sufficed quite so perfectly to be the finishing touch and the very zenith of all creation."[32]

What a concept! After all the creation of the world, the universe, and every living creature, God takes the time to specifically record the need for and the creation of womankind. Not only were we created in God's image with all the purposes

---

[32] MacArthur, John. *Twelve Extraordinary Women: How God Shaped Women of the Bible and What He Wants to Do with You.* Nashville, TN: Nelson Books, 2005. pp. 1–2.

that are found in that precious thought, but woman was also created with the flesh of another person. That was to signify the purpose that woman has to fulfill the needs of, and be companion for another created being, man.

"The zenith of all creation". Can we really claim that woman is that, the highest peak of all that God created in those six days of demonstrating his power and masterpiece? Interestingly enough, Paul the Apostle talks similarly about women in his first letter to the Corinthians. First Corinthians 11:7 reads: "For a man . . . is the image and glory of God, but woman is the glory of man." So, of all the creation, man was created in the image and glory of God and of that creation, which in itself is the highest of all creations, woman is the glory of that. So, not only is mankind created in the image of a holy, beautiful God, but also women specifically are called out to be a specific demonstration of the best of the best God has to offer. In a world that is looking for genuine demonstrations of God's character, power, and love, Christian women are called to give to them a demonstration of those attributes in the best and most-complete way possible. That includes our external appearance.

"It's about the heart," you might cry out in disagreement. After all, "the LORD sees not as man sees: man looks on the outward appearance, but the LORD looks on the heart."[33] While so often used as justification for the importance of inward character and a lack of necessary care for the outward, I would call attention to the verse in a new light. As God's creation and "image" on earth, we are called to be constantly pointing to him. As women, we are called even further to be the zenith of that representation and to demonstrate the best of his character and the greatest of his design. We would not have a necessity to do this if it weren't for the fact that "man looks on the outward appearance."

---

[33] 1 Samuel 16:7

We know how God views us as his creation. We know how he has shown his care to us; we do not need to demonstrate his majesty and his masterpiece to God himself. No, we are called to demonstrate this aspect of who God is to the world, mankind, around us. Therefore, since the Bible tells us that man looks at the external, we are called to use the external to demonstrate the character of God. We are again left without excuse. We are called to glorify God as his creation, as his temple, and also as his masterpiece. While we glorify him with the inner workings of his Son and Spirit in our hearts and souls (internal beauty), he also calls us to influence the world with a demonstration of his character through our externals.

Principles and Priorities

It can be overwhelming to look at the high calling God has given us as his children and furthermore as his daughters. It is not my intention to overwhelm but guide us as we take this task of honoring him with our external as well as our internal seriously.

Health

The beauty of what God has called us to is not cookie cutter. In the same way that God calls each and every person to a specific walk in life and does not instruct every believer to live exactly the same as another, God does not call every woman to the same size clothing, the same body measurements, nor the same number on a scale. Any ideology saying that a woman's beauty is measured by any of those factors would be in error. In actuality, what is taught through Scripture is the concept of true health. As we discussed earlier, God calls us to take care of his dwelling place, our bodies. He calls to us glorify him with what we do with it, and to "eat and drink" in a way that glorifies him. In order to understand what that means, it is important to understand the definition of "glorify God".

John Piper, in his sermon "God Created Us for His Glory", says this about what it means to bring glory to God: "Now, what then does it mean to say that God created us for his glory? Glory is a very hard thing to define. It is like the word 'Beauty.' . . . The glory of God is the beauty and excellence of his manifold perfections. It is an attempt to put into words what God is like in his magnificence and purity. It refers to his infinite and overflowing fullness of all that is good. The term might focus on his different attributes from time to time— like his power, and wisdom and mercy and justice—because each one is indeed awesome and beautiful in its magnitude and quality. But in general God's glory is the perfect harmony of all his attributes into one infinitely beautiful and personal being. Now when God says that he created us for his glory, it cannot mean that he created us so that he would become more glorious, that his beauty and perfection would be somehow increased by us. It is unthinkable that God should become more perfectly God by making something that is not God . . . . Instead what Isaiah 43:7 means is that he created us to display his glory, that is, glory might be known and praised." [34]

Glorifying God with our bodies, therefore, means to "display his glory that he might be known and praised" by the way we model his character. When 1 Corinthians 6:20 says to "glorify God with your bodies," it is a clear command to live in such a way that even our external attributes bring his name fame. Furthermore, we are called to live with a renewed understanding that glorifying God is giving our best that his fame might be spread.

---

[34] http://www.desiringgod.org/resource-library/sermons/god-created-us-for-his-glory

That might seem like a vague yet daunting task; but if we are honest with ourselves, we know enough about health and the treatment of our body to know what is healthy and what is not. We know that exercise is healthy—countless studies support this—and we know that the food we choose to eat can either assist us in being healthy or harm us, inadequately feed or unnecessarily over-fill the body in a way that is not best for its function.

I love to use my husband as an example in the discussion of health. Adam is 5'10" and 150 pounds on a good day. For him, it is a fight to gain weight and a missed meal can cause him to lose a pound (or more) in one day. He's been blessed with a very fast metabolism. To some people, he is the epitome of healthy, but in actuality, he struggles to eat healthily (he doesn't like most vegetables and can down a half-gallon of ice cream in two sittings), to get the necessary sleep required to fuel his body, and to find time to exercise. Just because his body *looks* like he is doing all the right things in order to be healthy, does not mean he *actually* is healthy. He would be the first to tell you that there is a difference between external appearance and actual health.

When Adam focuses on eating balanced meals with vegetables, getting adequate sleep, drinking water, and exercising faithfully, he can feel a difference in his body's performance on a day-to-day basis, and knows that his body is operating in a more productive, God-honoring way. Of course, most people don't have Adam's problem. For most of us, without the dedication of working out and eating well, we're not naturally fit. The lesson here is this: Whether or not you think you look the way you want, the motivation behind what we do with our bodies must be the glory of God and the spread of his fame to the ends of the earth.

I was never the exercise-focused child or teen. However, now that health and fitness are a very real and large area of my life, people have noticed the change. In fact, it has been quite the conversation starter. It has offered me opportunities to talk to people about the "why" behind my dedication, hard work, and insistence on prioritizing health and exercise in my life. While some of the obvious reasons for my desire to be healthy and fit find their source in my relationship with my husband, the heart behind what I do is and must continue to be to fulfill the calling of 1 Corinthians 6:20.

Glorifying God must be the heart behind the health we have internally with our spiritual walk, but it by no means excludes what we do with our outside temple. I would even go so far as to say that a woman who does not care about glorifying God with even the external (the most temporal of aspects of her life) and does not show care to bringing him glory with what the world sees of her every day will be guilty of disobedience to the Scripture. Furthermore, she will not be walking in the full blessing of sweet fellowship with Christ, and her internal health will suffer.

Yes, I do realize what a huge claim I made with that statement. I do not say it lightly. In fact, I sat here at my computer for a while watching the cursor dance until I reviewed all the Scriptures I have researched again. I find myself without excuse to glorify God with everything that I am, including my external, temporal body. Obviously, this works the other way as well: if your internal spiritual walk is not what it should be, your ability to glorify God with your temple is damaged significantly.

After all, Scripture repeats over and over the direct correlation between inward and outward health. Even in the Old Testament, we read passages such as Exodus 15:26 in which promises are made for the external health of the Israelites if they "diligently listen to the voice of the LORD your God, and do that which is right in his eyes." In the New Testament, John specifically mentions the health of his fellow believers in his prayers, saying, "Beloved, I pray that all may go well with you and that you may be in good health, as it goes well with your soul."[35] Here are some additional passages directly linking spiritual and physical health:

> Isaiah 58:11 "And the LORD will guide you continually and satisfy your desire in scorched places and make your bones strong; and you shall be like a watered garden, like a spring of water, whose waters do not fail."

Psalm 103:1–5 "Bless the LORD, O my soul, and all that is within me, bless his holy name! Bless the LORD, O my soul, and forget not all his benefits, who forgives all your iniquity, who heals all your diseases, who redeems your life from the pit, who crowns you with steadfast love and mercy, who satisfies you with good so that your youth is renewed like the eagle's."

Deuteronomy 28:2–4 "And all these blessings shall come upon you and overtake you, if you obey the voice of the LORD your God. Blessed shall you be in the city, and blessed shall you be in the field. Blessed shall be the fruit of your womb and the fruit of your ground and the fruit of your cattle, the increase of your herds and the young of your flock."

Psalm 32:3–4 "For when I kept silent, my bones wasted away through my groaning all day long. For day and night your hand was heavy upon me; my strength was dried up as by the heat of summer."

All these passages offer a direct correlation between physical and spiritual health. Not only can one have a direct effect on the other, in addition our calling as believers is to operate in a God-glorifying manner. That calling has inseparable responsibilities in both the external and internal. It is impossible to glorify God with one aspect of your life while willingly refusing to honor him in another.

---

[35]   3 John 1:2

Reprioritize

I want to challenge you in this: think back to when you first got saved. You were just rescued from the domination of Satan and his kingdom and welcomed into the family of a loving and holy God. Rescued and joyful, you found yourself with some need to reprioritize your life. Suddenly, you needed to be reading the Bible faithfully and taking the time to be in prayer. That required work. Then, part of your Sunday would be devoted to church and to learning and growing in what you were being taught. That required time. Then, you found yourself giving up certain activities (some of which you were still tempted to enjoy) because it meant throwing aside every weight, and sin which clings so closely in order to run with endurance the race that is set before you (paraphrase of Hebrews 12:1). That required sacrifice.

As we all look back on the time we've taken to be in the Word and to applying his teaching, growing in our prayer life, devoting ourselves to the people of God, and sacrificing to be obedient to what he's called us to, we realize that all that time, energy, commitment, discipline, and sacrifice have been worth it in order that we might better know Christ and his character and allow him to live in and through us. The health we have in our physical bodies is not much different. Taking back your health in order to bring glory to God through your external body will take time, effort, and sacrifice. However, Proverbs 14:23 makes this declaration: "In all toil there is profit" and the work put into dedicating your health to the Lord is no different.

While I desire to challenge you according to the biblical pattern we find in Scripture regarding the care to the external, let me remind the women who are "all or nothing" kind of personalities (like myself) that I am by no means putting care to the external as more important than the care to your spiritual well-being. We must prioritize and make sure that care is given to each and that we do not lose sight of the eternal in light of the temporal.

Pitfalls

When we start to put an emphasis on the need to "take back" our health, there are numerous pitfalls that arise as temptations placed by the devil and/or our sinful nature in order to distract us from our intended purpose. As mentioned earlier, our motivation for taking back our physical health must be rooted and grounded in a desire to bring glory and fame to God. Of course, as fallen creatures, we find ourselves distracted with other intentions—even those that are seemingly good. Those wayward desires capsize our "taking health back" boat and leave us unsatisfied, frustrated, disillusioned, and even obsessive. Temptations find us desiring the praise of men (or even just one man), comparing ourselves to other women, obsessing over a specific size/weight/measurement, or finding our worth in our externals.

Some may find fault in the activity and focus on health and fitness. I actually find issue with the pitfall and instead of throwing out the desire to be healthy and fit; I would challenge the heart of those pitfalls and address each with the answers that Scripture provides. Below, I have included a table that addresses some common temptations we face and verses that directly combat the heart behind that pitfall:

PITFALL	BIBLICAL COMBAT
Pleasing Man	Proverbs 29:25; Isaiah 2:22; John 12:43; Acts 5:29; 2 Corinthians 5:9; Galatians 1:10; Colossians 3:23; 1 Thessalonians 2:4
Obsessing Over Physical Appearance, Size, and Weight	1 Samuel 16:7; Jeremiah 17:5; Romans 8:1–17; 2 Peter 1:3

PITFALL	BIBLICAL COMBAT
Quitting/Throwing out Health	Proverbs 6:6–10, 21:25; Ecclesiastes 5:12, 11:6; Isaiah 40:29–31; Luke 12:48; 1 Corinthians 6:12–13, 20, 9:24–27; 2 Corinthians 12:9; 1 Timothy 4:12
Finding Our Worth in the Physical	1 Samuel 16:7; Jeremiah 17:5; John 5:44; Romans 8:1–17; 12:1–2; Galatians 2:20; Ephesians 2:8–9
Being Unsatisfied with Your Body as Designed by God	Genesis 1:27; Proverbs 139:13–16; Jeremiah 1:5; Matthew 10:31; Romans 8:32; 12:1–2; 1 Corinthians 10:13
Putting Physical Health as a Higher Priority than Spiritual Health	Jeremiah 17:5; Matthew 6:25–34; John 5:44; Romans 12:1–3; 1 Timothy 4:8

The issue here is not the concept of health and fitness. No, the issue is the sinful heart and lying devil, both of which twist a good thing into something that is self-seeking or man pleasing instead of God-glorifying.

<u>Physical</u> Limitations

Just as I want to be cautious and remember that we are faced with innumerable temptations and tendencies to give in to the pressures that society has put on women in the area of external beauty, I find it necessary to take the time to address another sensitive issue: physical limitations. Not every woman can be a runner. Some women have bad knees or other complications that make it impossible for them to go run a half marathon the way I enjoy. Other women have serious back, shoulder or other issues that keep them from being a lifter and doing strength training. Others are bound by wheelchairs and other more serious physical limitations that keep them from being very active at all. Having all women become an obsessive lover of working out is not my agenda for you as readers. This is not a commercial for a running club, a lifting program, or anything that necessarily looks like my exercise regime. No, this book is about your heart, about the responsibility you have as a Christian woman to honor the Lord and if you're married, to honor your husband. Remember, it's not about sizes, measurements, and pounds. It's about the heart.

My own grandmother was 500+ pounds. She had a thyroid problem. It would be unrealistic for me to expect that she would be able to do as much activity as other women, whether they were 300 pounds or 120 pounds. I by no means desire to put pressure on women who have serious and legitimate illnesses that keep them from being everything they desire to be physically. Believe me. I've been there. I was tested for thyroid issues just a couple of years ago. I know the struggle there is when the work you're putting in does not match up with the results you are seeing.

However, my grandmother also gave up. She was not always 500 pounds. She stopped trying. She had a lot of other things going on in her life, and instead of fighting for her own health, she let herself go. She stopped taking her medications and she stopped walking and exercising at all. She ate what she wanted and did what she wanted and she allowed her health to deteriorate to the point that she went into a diabetic coma and passed away at a rather young age. This is an extreme situation. This is not every woman's story, but it is a common temptation for women when faced with physical limitations that keep her from easily achieving the body that they'd desire.

If this is you—if you're faced with bodily limitations that keep you from progressing in the way you'd like—do not give up. Do not stop trying, stop eating healthy, or stop moving. Do what needs to be done in the area of seeking medical help for any complications that you have, and fight for your health. Your physical appearance is important, if only to give glory to God by offering him the best version of yourself—even when your best does not look like any other woman. Again, it's about the heart.

Balance

Perhaps you do not have a physical limitation. Perhaps the hard work pays off and you start achieving the look you've been fighting to have for so long. Perhaps you catch the workout bug and you find yourself loving every minute of being in the gym, on the treadmill, or out running the streets of your neighborhood. Perhaps you have started racing, competing as a lifter or Crossfit participant, and you are living for the next sporting event.

While I definitely have caught the workout bug, I cannot say that I have been 100% in the shoes of this kind of woman. I've not yet attained my ideal level of fitness. However, the attitude that drives me to that level and the heart behind my motivation for working out can easily fall into this category. While the woman with physical limitations finds herself wanting to give up, women who are hitting their stride in working out and seeing results often have the opposite temptation: obsession.

I truly desire that women make their external appearance a priority in their lives for the sole purpose of bringing glory to God. However, when the external appearance itself becomes an idol, we have lost the heart behind what we are called to do as women. We are out of balance. Balance looks different for each woman, as each woman's life course looks a little different from the next. However, we know enough about the life and heart of a godly woman according to Scripture to know that if exercise, fitness, and the externals in any way detour a woman's life from the priorities of serving Christ, glorifying him, spreading the word of salvation, serving the church, and honoring the Savior, things are out of balance. Balance—for one woman, that might look like avoiding 5k's that take her away from Sunday morning worship. For another, that might mean putting away the body builder's bikini because of the immodesty of that industry.

For another, and this is my life and probably more realistically yours, it means making the simple choice to run on the roads and lift weights at home instead of driving to a gym and paying for a gym membership. Or maybe you need the gym membership to keep you accountable, or even a trainer who will push you harder than you would push yourself. It means making the hard decision to put housework and service to my husband above my workout schedule and to ensure that only I feel the sacrifices made for this workout plan as much as possible, so that my family does not suffer.

Whatever challenge you are facing today, whether that of physical limitations or the temptation to become obsessed and imbalanced, I ask that you take some time to search your own heart and ask the Lord to reveal to you the ways you need to avoid giving up or to adjust your life to renew its balance. I truly believe if your heart is honestly seeking that, he will direct you.[36]

---

[36] Proverbs 3:5–6

CHAPTER 6

The Single Woman

I have to laugh sometimes when I think about my life now. The difference between Ashley today and Ashley in 1999 is enormous. I even laugh when I look back at Ashley as recently as 2008. I was a little bookworm, growing up as a tomboy, a lover of writing, and the one my mom long-called the least athletic in my family. I also hated science and told multiple people that I didn't care how my body worked, only that it worked properly. I was hardly a lover of health and nutrition.

Even as late as my junior year of college, I had only visited our campus gym twice. Once was to run on the treadmill—which lasted all of 20 minutes, of which I hated every minute and felt self-conscious. Another time was to drop off a paper for a friend who was there for work-study. I was hardly into fitness.

While I would like to say that I was challenged to give Christ my all and to start caring about my exterior for God's Glory, I cannot. It wasn't until I started dating my first boyfriend (now husband) that I made some changes. I realized that if he had been waiting 25 years for a wife, then it was my place to give him the best I could and honor his waiting for me. While my motivation was "sweet" and is still held close to my heart, I find some fatal flaws in my pre-dating motivations. Those flaws disturb me more than any changes I made in my lifestyle after he became important to me.

Christ the Groom

As a single woman, I had little care for my physical appearance. Don't get me wrong—I wanted to look good, to attract the attention of the right guys (and honestly, sometimes the wrong ones), and to be seen as physically beautiful. However, the perspective on being a steward of my external appearances for the glory of God was nowhere to be found. I had zero understanding of the responsibility I had before the Lord to honor him with my best—including my externals. While we've already talked in detail about the responsibility we have as God's creatures to give him glory with our externals as well as our internals, let us now take a look at another passage of Scripture that relates specifically to singles, externals, and the glory of God. First Corinthians 7:32–35 reads, "I want you to be free from anxieties. The unmarried man is anxious about the things of the Lord, how to please the Lord. But the married man is anxious about worldly things, how to please his wife, and his interests are divided. And the unmarried or betrothed woman is anxious about the things of the Lord, how to be holy in body and spirit. But the married woman is anxious about worldly things, how to please her husband. I say this for your own benefit, not to lay any restraint upon you, but to promote good order and to secure your undivided devotion to the Lord."

As a single person, I saw singleness as an excuse to not care about my body. After all, no one saw it but me, right? No one cared about what I looked like, right? I was not pleasing a man in marriage. After all, "God looks at the heart, right?"[37] What

---

[37]   1 Samuel 16:7

I did not realize, however, was that this passage does not say to disregard things that are important in marriage in order to be more holy in spirit alone as a single person. In fact, this passage is challenging the heart behind the motivations of such actions, both internal and external. Verse 34 says that the single woman is able to focus on "the things of the Lord, how to be holy *in body* and spirit" [emphasis added]. Even here, as a single man calling single men and women to focus solely on Christ, Paul challenges the readers to give their best of both body and spirit to the Lord. He is not calling single men and women to *not* care about the externals, as if a married partner were the only motivation for maintaining good health and fitness, but reminding both single and married believers that the motivation for everything needs to be Christ. This is more easily done when single and the motivation is truly to please the Lord completely, while a married person can be distracted from a pure motivation in an attempt to please one's spouse.

Therefore, the single woman, like the married woman, has the responsibility to maintain a healthy exterior in order to glorify and please her heavenly husband, Christ. Christ, the groom, desires holiness in his bride, the Church[38], and that holiness, according to 1 Corinthians 7, includes the external body as well as the internal spirit. In the same way that a married person is set apart for one person as their spouse in a covenant before the Lord, the body of a single person can be made holy unto the Lord. In fact, "holiness" and "marriage" are actually the same word in the Hebrew language.[39] This reinforces that the covenant made between a man and a woman in matrimony and the relationship between a single woman and the Lord is similar. Therefore, when Paul calls single women to be "holy in body and spirit," he is

---

[38] Ephesians 5:25–27; Revelation 19:7–9

[39] http://site.themarriagebed.com/bible/what-the-bible-says/coveant-a-marriage/is-marriage-a-covenant

challenging the unmarried woman to view her life as "married" to Christ in the way she deals with her body (externals) and spirit (internals).

So, there I was, living my own single life with my unhealthy food, lack of exercise, gluttony, and laziness, not devoted at all to my spiritual groom. I spent time developing my spiritual (internal) devotion to the Lord, but never realized the responsibility I had to offer my body to my divine groom with the same fervor.

Preparation for Marriage

While the previous section describes the heartbeat and purpose for single women and their view of the externals, I would like to motivate you in another manner as well. When Adam and I started dating, my lifestyle changed drastically. As I began to consider how much of a privilege it was to have a virgin as a soon-to-be husband, I also began to realize the joy it would be to share our bodies with each other for the very first time. While I desired to be loved for more than my externals, I realized that physical attraction played an important part of the marriage relationship. I knew it was important. I had a small idea of the struggles any single man would face in this sex-crazed world. As a result, I wanted to offer him something beautiful as a way of saying "thank you" for his dedication to waiting for me.

You might be single with no man in sight. Right now, you have a spiritual groom in Christ. However, if you desire to be married one day, then you can honor your husband by what you do with your body even now. You may not have a timeline to a wedding dress or a wedding night, but the work you do now will honor him then and show him gratitude for the love he will show you. In the same way that healthy eating and exercising have benefits for the future of the function of your physical body, what you do with your health and fitness today can express love and appreciation to a man in the future.

Too often women behave as I did, and suddenly, when a man enters their life, they find it important to make drastic life changes in order to have the "perfect" body by the wedding night. This often leads to imbalance, frustration, and a lack of healthy decisions that are not lifestyle changes to be kept over a lifetime. They are rash decisions that can have negative lifelong results. In 2012, ABC News released a story about the new K-E wedding diet that had women using feeding tubes in order lose 10–20 pounds in the last 10-day stretch before their wedding day. The tubed process was designed to drastically limit calorie intake (800 calories total per day) and send the body into ketosis to burn body fat.[40] Still, others try the more drastic anorexic and bulimic trends in an attempt to unhealthily accomplish in a short amount of time what a few months or years of focus on health and nutrition could have accomplished naturally and healthily.

So, with God's glory as our ultimate focus and health as the practical way that we can glorify him with our externals, I challenge you, as a single woman, to plan to honor your potential future husband through your body without damaging it for a lifetime. I challenge you to offer your body first to Christ, your spiritual groom. Then plan for an earthly groom by making the life changes that need to happen now, before you are tempted to make those changes in an unhealthy manner.

---

[40] http://abcnews.go.com/Health/diet-brides-feeding-tubes-rapidly-shed-pounds/story?id=16146271

CHAPTER 7

Modesty

It is important in any discussion of externals to mention the tendency that women have to not only be attractive physically but to put those externals on display. We want to be recognized as beautiful by men and women alike. The temptation is to show skin (or to wear skin-tight clothing) in order to prove to the world that we are indeed beautiful. In this section, we will discuss the necessity women have to remain modest. Modest. It is such a subjective word, having been defined and re-defined countless times over the centuries. At one point in history, a woman wearing pants was considered immodest. At other times (and even in some current cultures), a woman wearing anything (even a skirt or dress) shorter than the ankles was considered scandalous. So, let us take a look at the biblical heart of modesty.

The Bible does not distinguish between modesty for a married woman versus that for a single woman; the verses that address modesty simply address women as a whole. Some of the most popular references include 1 Timothy 2:9, which says, "Likewise also that women should adorn themselves in respectable apparel, with modesty and self-control, not with braided hair and gold or pearls or costly attire." 1 Peter 3:3–4 further states, "Do not let your adorning be external—the braiding of hair and the putting on of gold jewelry, or the clothing you wear— but let your adorning be the hidden person of the heart with the imperishable beauty of a gentle and quiet spirit, which in God's sight is very precious."

Of course, the mere presence of the word "modesty" in 1 Timothy does not assist us in the explanation of this word. In order to fully understand what modesty means and the heart of the Lord in giving women this mandate, let's take a closer look at the full counsel of Scripture as it pertains to a woman's body, its use, its clothing, and yes, its power over the male gender.

In Proverbs, we read a wealth of verses warning men about the wiles of the seductive woman. Often, they refer to the manner in which the woman is dressed (Proverbs 5–7). In Genesis 38:14–15, Judah judges a woman by how she looks and considers her a prostitute simply by her appearance (and it turns out to be his own daughter-in-law!). Even from the beginning of the Bible, we are given numerous examples of women who have used clothing to entice men for sexual purposes. Therefore, it is important to study this issue of clothing and external appearance; Scripture demonstrates them as being both influential in the view others have on a woman as well as a part of woman's important responsibility before God and man.

C.J. Mahaney, in his book *Worldliness: Resisting the Seduction of a Fallen World*, defines modesty is the following way: "Modesty means propriety. It means avoiding clothes and adornment that are extravagant or sexually enticing. Modesty is humility expressed in dress. It's a desire to serve others, particularly men, by not promoting or provoking sensuality. Immodesty, then, is much more than wearing a short skirt or low-cut top; it's the act of drawing undue attention to yourself. It's pride, on display by what you wear. Self-control is, in a word, restraint. Restraint for the purpose of purity; restraint for the purpose of exalting God and not ourselves. Together, these attitudes of modesty and self-control should be the hallmark of the godly woman's dress."[41]

I like this definition simply because it is not about a specific standard of dress. Modesty is not about the length of one's skirt, the amount of cleavage showing, the tightness of one's outfit, and the percentage of skin showing. Modesty, like so many of the topics we have been discussing, is an issue of the woman's heart: her understanding of the purpose of her body before God, and her desire to fulfill the responsibility she has to be modest before men.

Protection

Whether single or married, we all want to be recognized for our beauty. As we develop inner character, we understand the importance of the "inner beauty" we demonstrate through our lifestyles and personality, but the external still remains important to us. We know the importance of giving God glory with our externals and of offering him our very best, we now need to learn how to avoid causing men to stumble in the process.

We can begin to understand the struggle men face every day with the "desires of the eyes"[42] by examining the verses addressed to them regarding lustful thoughts and images. Matthew 5:28 challenges men to avoid looking at women in a way that is lustful; "But I say to you that everyone who looks at a woman with lustful intent has already committed adultery with her in his heart." Psalm 119:37 is the prayer of one man and an example for all men who desire freedom from visual temptations; "Turn my eyes from looking at worthless things; and give me life in your ways." 2 Timothy 2:22 is a well-known challenge to men to flee

---

[41] http://www.sovereigngraceministries.org/blogs/cj-mahaney/post/2008/04/25/Modesty-The-Attitude-of-the-Modest-Woman-(pt-2).aspx

[42] 1 John 2:16

lust and to pursue Christ; "So flee youthful passions and pursue righteousness, faith, love, and peace, along with those who call on the Lord from a pure heart."

Statistics and modern studies also show us the power that visuals have over men. The Center for Behavioral Neuroscience did a study on the differences between the emotional and motivational responses of men and women when shown images. The activity in the brain and body of man was highly different, and much more active, than that of the woman[43]. We'll talk about this in more detail in chapter ten.

We know that men are called to personal responsibility in these matters. I am by no means excusing a man who struggles with keeping his mind pure in what he thinks about or views. However, my desire is for women to become more knowledgeable regarding the differences between what we might consider a struggle or problem and what men actually struggle with on a day-to-day basis. It is necessary to recognize that just because this area may not be an intense struggle for all women does not change the reality that men do struggle in a more intense way. Therefore, I point women to the following verses that speak to the responsibility we have to our fellow brothers in Christ: to assist in guarding them from sin and to avoid being a cause of temptation/sin in their lives.

In 1 Thessalonians 4:3–8, specifically, we see Paul talk first to the men of Christ and remind them of their personal responsibility: "For this is the will of God, your sanctification: that you abstain from sexual immorality; that each one of you know how to control his own body in holiness and honor, not in the passion of lust like the Gentiles who do not know God," but he does not stop there. Immediately following this, Paul instructs us "that no one transgress and wrong his brother in this matter, because the Lord is an avenger in all these things, as we told you

---

[43] http://www.sciencedaily.com/releases/2004/03/040316072953.htm

beforehand and solemnly warned you. For God has not called us for impurity, but in holiness. Therefore whoever disregards this, disregards not man but God, who gives his Holy Spirit to you."

Notice the warning here is not only to men (although they are warned in other passages of God's judgment for impurity), but also to women who would disregard the struggle of their fellow brothers in Christ, because God is a God of justice. As if the reminder that God is a "an avenger in all these things" was not enough, be reminded of the judgment of God stated in Romans 2:6–8, which says, "He will render to each one according to his works: to those who by patience in well-doing seek for glory and honor and immortality, he will give eternal life; but for those who are self-seeking and do not obey the truth, but obey unrighteousness, there will be wrath and fury."

Additional passages regarding causing a brother to stumble include 1 Corinthians 8:9, Mark 9:42, and Romans 14:1–23—all of which include real examples of the responsibility we have to guard the hearts of our fellow believers in all areas, including those as seemingly inconsequential as food and holidays. How much more so in the area of sexual purity?

Potential – The Single Woman

As a single woman, the externals seem more straightforward. I remember as a single woman thinking that if I wasn't attractive, I would never catch the right one's eye. Let's be honest: we've all felt that way! We want to be seen as beautiful, to be desired, and to be the one the right man wants to be with. While I would agree that externals are important in the chase between a man and a woman before marriage, I would counsel all single women to honor any potential husband God could provide by being modest in their appearance.

I will never forget the impact reading Jennifer Lamp's book *His Chosen Bride* had on me as a young teen. For the first time ever, I studied through Proverbs 31 and saw the responsibility that married women had to fulfill the character qualities of the woman in that passage but also the ability that I had as a single woman to possess those same qualities while unmarried! Of course, this was just a hint to the heart attitude that it takes to be a godly wife— which is first cultivated in the heart and life of a single woman, years before she says her wedding vows.

One of the most impactful sections of the book involved Proverbs 31:12, which reads: "She does him good, and not harm, all the days of her life." This is how Jennifer challenges single women: "Okay, so let's say that God does have marriage planned for you. It has been said that God is more concerned about our marriage than we are! What can you do today that would do your future husband good? What skills can you learn? How should you treat other young men you meet? What areas of character might break the spirit of a marriage? . . . It is interesting to notice our chapter's verse says she will do him good, 'all the days of her life' rather than 'from the time they get married' or even 'once they meet.' For us this means . . . we can be doing that husband good today, even if he is yet unknown."[44] Wow, is that not life-changing? You, yes, you, the single woman with no potential husband on the horizon, can affect his life and bring him good even now! This includes how you dress before other men and what you do with your body and health.

Growing up, my mom would give us the analogy of a piece of gum when referring to physical purity and our wedding day. My mom would say to us that having sex with anyone before your wedding night is like offering a piece of gum to someone, letting

---

[44] Lamp, Jennifer J. *His Chosen Bride: Living out Your Position as Daughter of the King and Bride of Christ.* Wichita, KS: Grace Works Ministry Press, 2000. pp. 52–53

them open it up, smell it, and chew it. Then, when marriage comes, it's taking that same piece of gum and offering it to the man you are making a vow to marry—pre-chewed. As a young child, and even now, that visual picture is disgusting. If I love my husband—even if I don't know him yet!—there is no way I want to arrive at our wedding night with a pre-chewed piece of gum as my only gift to him. No, I want to keep my gum safely in its package, so he can be the first and only one to enjoy it, rich in its entire flavor and without the disgusting results of being pre-chewed.

Perhaps it's too late for you. Am I calling you disgusting and only worthy of being thrown out? God forbid. That is the beauty of forgiveness and grace. It is about what you do from this day forward, not about living in the past, held down by guilt and regrets. Move forward in confidence that God restores!

I would further encourage you not only to not let other men "chew" on your physical beauty in actual sexual relations, but also in refusing to allow men to diminish your beauty in any way that cheapens the sweetness of your gift to your husband at the altar. For example, I would also apply this to what we do with our modesty and how much skin we put on display for the whole world to see. To expand, taking the gum analogy a step further, allowing the whole world to view what your husband will one day have all the right to view in its natural, naked beauty, is to buy a pack of gum for someone but to allow anyone to handle those pieces of gum, open the packages, smell them, and fondle them, so that, although not eaten, they are not in their best, original shape when they are offered to the intended receiver.

Pride – The Married Woman

Perhaps you are married. On your wedding night, you gave the man of your dreams the gift of your body, saved and protected, unshared. Your responsibility to honor him and protect him does not end at the exchange of the marriage vows. When a woman accepts the gift of salvation, makes a vow to love Christ, and devotes her life to serving him in everything, there is no sharing involved with the sinful nature. While her flesh might rage against her, the intent believer commits everything she has to "throwing off" the old and "putting on" the new in order to bring the most glory and honor to Christ.

Marriage, the earthly representation of Christ and the Church[45], needs to operate the same way. You and your husband have made sacred vows to one another "for better or worse," "in sickness and in health," and "to have and to hold… 'til death do [you] part." In that vow is the underlying promise to remain faithful to one another through whatever comes. Like the commitment you make to Christ, who offers no caveat for sharing his glory or his pride with mankind in any way[46], marriage offers no excuse for sharing with the world what belongs to your covenanted spouse.

Confession: I love my bikinis. I will admit that I own more than my fair share. I like them in different styles, colors, shapes, and sizes. I also love miniskirts. However, although I would love to wear miniskirts all the time and bikinis at every pool I visit, I choose not to wear these items in public for a variety of reasons. The first reason is the responsibility I have to guard my brothers in Christ from the temptation in sin. The second reason is that while my husband enjoys me in bikinis and short skirts, he does not like me wearing those in public. As a result, I respect my husband and desire to honor him by not showing off to the world what is his alone to enjoy.

It is the temptation of women to declare that our bodies are our own and what we do or do not wear is of no one else's concern.

---

45   Ephesians 5:21–32
46   Isaiah 42:8

Our husband, we think, should not determine what we wear. If we are comfortable in public, he can just get over it. However, this could not be further from the truth. First Corinthians 7:4 reads, "For the wife does not have authority over her own body, but the husband does." It is important to notice that this covenant of marriage involves physical purity as well as godly jealousy.

Scripturally, we see God declares himself a jealous God (Exodus 20:5; 34:14), protective of what is his own. In the same way, men are rightfully jealous over what is their own (their wife and their wife's body). Not caring to understand this is to disregard your covenant before God and your spouse, to throw out passages such as 1 Corinthians 7 and Ephesians 5, and to forget that the whole purpose of marriage is to act as an image of Christ and the church. It is right for your husband to desire to be the only one to enjoy your nakedness, in the same way that God is jealous to be the Church's one and only (Ezekiel 16, 23–24). Simply put, as man is the image and glory of Christ[47], so you are your husband's pride. You are his and his alone. He might like how you look in a variety of outfits, but discretion must be given and modesty considered in order to protect what is for his eyes only.

---

[47] 1 Corinthians 11:7

CHAPTER 8

The Married Woman

We have now talked about a variety of external beauty topics in relation to the lives of women in general. We know that external beauty is important—all mankind is the image and glory of Christ and women are the apex of creation. We know that singleness is no excuse for external neglect because Christ is our spiritual groom and we can honor a future husband through what we do today with our body. However, more often than not the issue of women "letting themselves go" is not as much about the single woman as it about the married woman. She has allowed a variety of distractions to sidetrack her from her responsibility to fulfill her purpose as a wife within the marriage relationship. We will now focus on what those responsibilities are before God and before the man that you have committed to love. External appearance is a vital and biblical part of the vows you have made to both.

Fulfilling Your Purpose

Creation Generally

Mankind was not created like any other creature. Scooped from the dirt of God's creation and breathed into, the first human bore the image of God in a way no plant, bug, sea animal, flying beast, or mammal ever did (or ever will). God created a being to be a physical representation of himself on earth. This creation demonstrated God's care and character, his creativity, and his perfect design. Thousands of years later, Jesus came to earth to demonstrate God's love to those he had created. Jesus showed love in the most extreme way possible[48] and offered himself as an example for believers to follow from that day forward.

The same God who designed mankind from the dirt and created woman from the rib of a man is the same God who found it important and in his perfect design to present himself *in the flesh* to die for mankind in a visual picture of the love he has for his creation. This same God designed marriage and the roles of men and women in the marriage covenant to mirror the love story he has between him and the creation he loves so dearly.

This affects women practically in our care of the external in this way: God has designed men to represent Christ in the relationship. In Ephesians 5, Paul writes under the inspiration of the Holy Spirit to men about their role in this divine imagery: "Husbands, love your wives, as Christ loved the church and gave himself up for her, that he might sanctify her, having cleansed her by the washing of water with the word, so that he might present the church to himself in splendor, without spot or wrinkle or any such thing, that she might be holy and without blemish. In the same way husbands should love their wives as their own bodies. He who loves his wife loves himself. For no one ever

---

[48] John 15:13

hated his own flesh, but nourishes and cherishes it, just as Christ does the church, because we are members of his body. 'Therefore a man shall leave his father and mother and hold fast to his wife, and the two shall become one flesh.'"[49]

In that same chapter, Christian women are called to the divine role of responding to Christ in the same way that God has called the Church to respond to him: "Wives, submit to your own husbands, as to the Lord. For the husband is the head of the wife even as Christ is the head of the church, his body, and is himself its Savior. Now as the church submits to Christ, so also wives should submit in everything to their husbands." While this is a general command to respond to your husband in the same way that you as a believer are called to respond to Christ, we do not see a direct command that says to "care about your appearance for your husband's sake." However, we are called to offer Christ our best, to glorify him, which, simply put, is to make him look great before the world. While our husbands are not to be worshipped as we would worship Christ, we are called to honor our husbands and to glorify them before men. This is evidenced in Ephesians, not to mention a variety of other passages including Proverbs 12:4 and the well-loved Proverbs 31. In the same way, 2 Corinthians 5:20 calls the church "ambassadors for Christ". If we are to represent the relationship between Christ and the church, we should also view ourselves as our husband's "ambassadors" or "representatives".

Amidst the verses talking about the virtuous woman in Proverbs 31, we run across verse 23, which reads: "Her husband is known in the gates, when he sits among the elders of the land." We can stand back and wonder how this random verse falls into the description of a godly woman. But it is not random—it is through the honor and respect that a godly wife gives to her

---

[49] Ephesians 5:23–31

husband that he has gained his reputation. She has become known for her character, which is a reflection of his character.

Therefore, before the ungodly world in which we find ourselves, before an ungodly generation that has thrown out gender roles and any semblance of biblical marriage, let your marriage and your role in it be something resembling Christ and his bride, the Church. The rubber hits the road right here. Which is more honoring to your husband? A woman who pays attention to what she looks like and how healthy and fit she is, or the woman who has let herself go? If you are anything like women I know, we talk about the men we know and the pairings we see. Somehow, whether we like it or not, we do find ourselves evaluating couples by their exteriors and their combinations by the care they put into the way they carry themselves.

In the book *For Women Only*, the author Shaunti Feldhahn took a survey of men from a variety of walks of life and found amazing statistics about how men view the looks of their wives as direct reflections on them as men. One man honestly shared: "Those women need to realize that their doubling in size is like a man going from being a corporate raider to a minimum-wage slacker—and assuming it has no effect on his spouse. A woman's appearance is a simple yet important part of happiness in a marriage."[50] Another shared that "Every man has this innate competition with other men, and our wives are a part of that. Every man wants other men to think that he did well."[51] The findings are interesting, challenging, and humbling. They directly walk hand-in-hand with the understanding of our role as the Church before the spiritual groom, Christ, and the image we display here on earth through the covenant of marriage.

---

[50]   Feldhahn, Shaunti. *For Women Only: What You Need to Know about the Inner Lives of Men.* Sisters, Or.: Multnomah Publishers, 2004. pp. 166–167

[51]   Feldhahn, Shaunti. *For Women Only: What You Need to Know about the Inner Lives of Men.* Sisters, Or.: Multnomah Publishers, 2004. pp. 168–169

I then ask you to do this very hard task: to first set your heart on the importance you have as God's creation and the responsibility you have before Christ and your husband to represent Jesus Christ and the Church, both to the world and to your husband.

Women Specifically

Take the time to pray before continuing through this section. I will forewarn you that this section is not politically correct nor is it easy for the pride-filled heart of a sinner to hear. It's not easy to write either. The topic of the creation of women has been discussed as the apex of God's creation. We were the last created being, the only being created from a living being, and the only creation specifically designed to meet a need.

It is this last understanding that I seek to address now. In all the narrative of creation, there is one creation that God does not immediately call "good" upon completion. Take a look at Genesis 2:5–8 and 15–18: "When no bush of the field was yet in the land and no small plant of the field had yet sprung up—for the LORD God had not caused it to rain on the land, and there was no man to work the ground, and a mist was going up from the land and was watering the whole face of the ground— then the LORD God formed the man of dust from the ground and breathed into his nostrils the breath of life, and the man became a living creature. And the LORD God planted a garden in Eden, in the east, and there he put the man whom   he had formed. . . . The LORD God took the man and put him in the garden of Eden to work it and keep it. And the LORD God commanded the man, saying, 'You may surely eat of every tree of the garden, but of the tree of the knowledge of good and evil you shall not eat, for in the day that you eat of it you shall surely die.' Then the LORD God said, 'It is not good that the man should be alone . . . '"

The God of all creation has named all things good—until now. He does not declare this newest, most-intricate creation of man "good." He actually states the opposite when he says, "It is not good." Subsequently, there was a need for another creation, so God formed woman from the rib of man. While the understanding of woman as the final creation can offer us confidence in the beauty of our creation and the pre-sin perfection God intended for this design, examine another angle of this understanding: without woman, man is incomplete. The imagery is clear in the actual formation of woman from a part of man (the removal of his rib). More significantly, it is clear in God's reaction to creation as incomplete before the presence of woman in the man's life. And then he declares it good (or complete) following his design of a creation to meet that need. Yes, you, as a woman, were created to meet a need.

I do not seek to make our position of "help-meet" appear demeaning or to call ourselves objects before men. However, I want to again appeal to you as not only a wife, but first and foremost as the creation of a wise and holy God. Before you allow your pride to well up and distract you from the beauty of the creation of woman herself, let us be reminded of Isaiah 45:9. This passage confronts those creatures who would think in their futility that they know better than the plan of the designer: "Woe to him who strives with him who formed him, a pot among earthen pots! Does the clay say to him who forms it, 'What are you making?'" No, we have no excuse to answer back to God, in our pride, and say he is unjust or unfair in any way for creating women as those who meet needs.

Romans 9:20–23 goes into greater detail, "But who are you, O man, to answer back to God? Will what is molded say to its molder, 'Why have you made me like this?' Has the potter no right over the clay, to make out of the same lump one vessel for honorable use and another for dishonorable use? What if God, desiring to show his wrath and to make known his power, has endured with much patience vessels of wrath prepared for destruction, in order to make known the riches of his glory for vessels of mercy, which he has prepared beforehand for glory." There you have it. While we, as lumps of created clay, might be tempted to answer back to the Potter and challenge his design for women, let us focus on the second portion of that passage. It declares the creature as designed to "make known his power," whatever the intended purpose of the vessel.

We, as mankind and specifically women, have been created for God's glory. We are called to spread his fame and will never experience true satisfaction unless we are fulfilling our intended purpose. We will never be truly happy unless we are bringing God honor by making known the "riches of his glory" through the role he has created first of all for us as humans and secondly as women. As a married woman, we will never be as fulfilled in our marriage as when we walk as the completion of the man to which you have made your vows.

This is a powerful position given to us. We are broken, sinful people, and yet God has entrusted to us the blessing and responsibility to aid our husbands in their ability to glorify God. After all, on his own, he is not fully complete. It is the addition of you into his life that will better enable him to bring God glory and turn was incomplete into something "good" in the eyes of the perfect designer and creator.

This has not always been a widely understood thought. We have probably heard teachings on our role as "help-meet" to our husband and on how to assist our husbands, but it has often been twisted as a guilt-ridden challenge to women to realize our rank before and under men. I believe that is why this understanding raises the hair on the back of many women's necks. This belief in our "place" as under men is one that has been twisted and used by male chauvinists and those who do not understand the beauty of God's creation story. Understand that there is freedom and joy found in walking in the understanding of his need for you, not his power over you. You are not below him in leadership as a means of degradation (1 Corinthians 11). It is for your own protection (Genesis 3). In fact, you have a great responsibility to assist him in his walk before the Lord. You are the woman who is most influential in meeting his needs before God.

With a renewed understanding of the special role God has given to you as a wife, we will be addressing the variety of ways in which you can assist him in his role before God. While the avenues for influence are endless, the remainder of this book will address the responsibility you have to utilize your physical appearance to assist your husband in fulfilling his role before God, keeping his vows to you, protecting his heart and mind in purity, and growing as a team so you might together glorify God to the best of your ability.

CHAPTER 9

Reverse Roles

When I reached this point in the writing process, I felt a sigh of relief. Of all the chapters I have written so far, I have been the most excited to address the topic of reverse roles. Don't get me wrong—what we have talked about up until now is the heart of beauty both internal and external. Without the former chapters, we would still have no motivation (or at most, we'd have an incorrect motivation) for the actions and perspectives needed by both single and married women. But what follows is the heart of this woman.

I am not a perfect example of loving your husband in a way that completes him and fulfills all his needs in a biblical fashion. I am not saying, like Paul, "follow me." I am still learning and growing in this area as well. Hopefully growing more as I understand more deeply the calling I have before God as his daughter and before my husband as his bride.

I've done a lot of praying and talking with my husband as we've worked through the process of this book. While my hands have been on the keyboard creating the combinations of words and sentences, this book is truly a compilation of numerous discussions, questions, study, and purposeful research. We've attempted to understand men, men's view of beauty, women, the world's expectations, and most importantly, what the Scripture has to say about our need to honor the Lord with our whole health, both spiritual and physical.

As we turn the corner from addressing the heart to looking at how those heart decisions affect our day-to-day lives, let's discuss expectations. While we could likely find excuses based in the unrealistic expectations that society has put on women—demanding from us a level of external beauty we are supposedly able to attain—women are without excuse before God. It would be wrong to assume that all male expectations are unbiblical and selfish. In fact, we would be unrealistic and blind if we didn't realize that women have their own expectations on their husbands that, to them, can seem just as unrealistic or unbiblical—while we find them completely reasonable.

Let's get personal. Even as a strikingly practical and hardly sentimental woman, I find myself with expectations for my husband that I find realistic, reasonable, and proper. For instance, while Adam may or may not necessarily feel a need to talk about his day when he gets home, I expect a certain amount of reasonable conversation about our days. I expect him to ask about my day and to show care for what my life has been like since I've seen him last. I expect him to listen to me tell stories about insignificant events, drama at work, or blog posts I'm considering. I expect some level of assistance. Sure, he's worked all day, but so have I. I expect a little help here and there: taking out the garbage, changing the oil in the car, and whatever else needs to be done to help our lives run smoothly.

I have sexual expectations for Adam as well. Since we're talking about married women and our relationships with our husbands, let me be honest and open enough to say that I have expectations that involve both my emotional and physical needs. I expect him to care about meeting those needs, whether they are immediate desires of his or whether he agrees with my understanding of them as necessities.

As a mother, I have additional expectations. I expect that Adam will be interested in the growth, health, and care of our sons. I expect that he will want to spend time with Titus and Logan even after a long day at work. I expect him to show our sons love and "train up [our children] in the way [they] should go."[52]

These are reasonable expectations, yes? I can honestly and objectively look at these expectations and say that I am only expecting him to be what he has been called to in Scripture. He has been called to lead, love, serve, and cherish me as his wife. It may be well and good to hear confirmation about the *reasonable* (please note the emphasis I have on that word) expectations we have for our spouses. However, the point of this chapter is not to affirm the expectations that we have for our men, but to open our eyes to the fact that those normal expectations that we have may not come naturally to him to fulfill.

For example, your expectation for your husband to meet your emotional needs will not be something he views as his highest priority. It is unnatural to him. While, of course, this is making a rather large generalization, men are much less emotional creatures than women. Just think about it. We can have our emotional times of the day (due to being tired or stressed). We even have a whole week devoted to a time when our emotions can run wild as we have "hormonal issues" during our menstrual cycle. Men do not run into these same emotional roller coasters and their hormones do not affect their emotions in the same way. However, despite this being a rather foreign concept to men, we expect them to at least have patience with us in our times of great emotion. It's not natural for him, but we expect him to learn that it is important to us and to accommodate those needs.

Let's reverse roles. In the same way that you have a variety of expectations for your husband that do not seem natural to him, he also has expectations of you. I want to challenge your heart in this

---

[52] Proverbs 22:6

as we look at those expectations, and as we have just discussed, we see they are not all wrong or out-of-place. As a married man, your husband might have expectations about your involvement around the house. He might expect you to be the one to do the laundry, dishes, and food preparation. He might expect you to do most of the childcare or numerous other tasks that he views as "the woman's job." Whether or not these are realistic is not the point. Carefully examine your heart. If it's anything like mine, you might find yourself intensely upset that anyone, even your husband, should have expectations about you, your work level, and your responsibilities. Do you not have the same expectations of him, simply in different areas?

Let's look a little closer at those other expectations to which I have alluded. Like I hinted at earlier, I have emotional and sexual needs. I'm a woman who loves her man's physical touch. I do not think it is unrealistic to expect his attention to my needs before, during, and after we make love. It is not unreasonable to expect that when we are making love, he will help me sexually and give care to meeting my needs, no matter how foreign those needs are to his own, no matter how much additional work that makes for him in the process, etc. In the same way, he has expectations regarding his sexual needs, and [brace yourself] they involve your physical appearance. While this seems like a simple concept, take note that your man is a visual creature. Your ability to completely please him and satisfy him sexually, although not dependent on your body, is greatly assisted by what he sees with his eyes.

While you know that you are not the only woman with emotional needs, somehow it is harder for us to accept that this universal male expectation of physical attraction has any real basis. You might think, "What? It's not just my husband's issue?" No, we are all resigned to this truth. Your husband has certain expectations that he will find your body sexually appealing. While his expectations cannot be based on unrealistic fantasies, it would be wrong for women to look at the man God has given us and expect him to operate in a way other than how God has designed him to work.

Let's reverse roles again. You and your husband are kissing. He strips off his shirt and down to his boxers and then stands and flexes his muscles. He poses and teases you with glimpses of his body. Then, he sits back down to continue kissing and expects you to be ready to make love. Is that a realistic expectation? Perhaps you are a highly visual woman or you are easily turned on, but for a majority of women what is required is much more than a visual show. It takes care, work, time, direction, and emotional unity to prepare us for the marriage bed. Yes, we are complicated creatures when it comes to love. In the same way, it would be ludicrous for a husband to think that a little extra skin could arouse his wife, it is unrealistic to think that only technically "meeting his sexual needs" is fully loving him and serving him the way God has called wives.

Perhaps you think I am exaggerating the visual aspect of our husbands. Perhaps you think that even if I am right, that his expectation is still unrealistic or unbiblical. There are numerous passages in Scripture in which kings and men of old took notice of the external beauty of a woman (Abraham, Isaac, Jacob, King David, King Solomon, King Xerxes, King Herod, etc.). Let us address some of the passages in Song of Solomon that directly involve the beauty of the bride as viewed by the groom:

> "Behold, you are beautiful, my love,
> behold, you are beautiful!
> Your eyes are doves behind your veil.
> Your hair is like a flock of goats
> leaping down the slopes of Gilead . . . .
> Your neck is like the tower of David,
> built in rows of stone; on it hang a thousand shields,
> all of them shields of warriors.
> Your two breasts are like two fawns,

twins of a gazelle, that graze among the lilies.
Until the day breathes and the shadows flee,
I will go away to the mountain of myrrh
and the hill of frankincense.
You are altogether beautiful, my love;
there is no flaw in you. . . .
How beautiful is your love, my sister, my bride!
How much better is your love than wine,
and the fragrance of your oils than any spice!
Your lips drip nectar, my bride;
honey and milk are under your tongue;
the fragrance of your garments is like the fragrance of Lebanon.
A garden locked is my sister, my bride,
a spring locked, a fountain sealed . . . .
Your rounded thighs are like jewels,
the work of a master hand.
Your navel is a rounded bowl
that never lacks mixed wine.
Your belly is a heap of wheat,
encircled with lilies.
Your two breasts are like two fawns,
twins of a gazelle.
Your neck is like an ivory tower.
Your eyes are pools in Heshbon,
by the gate of Bath-rabbim. . . .
Oh may your breasts be like clusters of the vine,
and the scent of your breath like apples,
and your mouth like the best wine."[53]

Uncomfortable yet? This biblical book offers us numerous examples of how this one man found beauty in the physical appearance of the bride of his youth. Now, tell me, does your

---

[53]   Song of Solomon 4:1, 4–7, 10–12; 7:1b–4a, 8b–9a

man find as much beauty in your physical appearance? I am not debating expectations that are unreasonable, unrealistic, or unhealthy. I am not giving license to sin in the hearts of men. I am simply calling women to a higher standard than the one we so often hold for ourselves. I am asking you to take a moment to look at the heart of your man as if it were your own—how would it make you feel if your emotional and womanly needs were not met?

Take time to reverse the roles in your mind. Think through the marriage books that you have read where you may have found yourself desiring a highlighter and a listening husband so you could emphasize *your* needs in a way he might understand. Think through the countless times you have tried to express your needs to him and found him clueless, unable to understand the topic of hurt and how it was such a sensitive and important issue to you. Think through those times you have cried and your patient but tentative man was afraid to ask what was wrong.

These hurts and pains and failed expectations have often landed couples in marriage counseling, with the goal of the husband better knowing his wife's needs and being like Christ to her by meeting those needs and loving her as he ought.

Now, take those same emotions and feelings, hurts, pains, expectations, and disappointments. Realize how possibly, just possibly, your neglect of your external beauty has been the equivalent of his callous words spoken to you, or his lack of care to your emotional needs, or his failure to communicate plans, or his lack of a desire or care to meet your physical needs, or whatever pain has arisen in your mind. Your lack of care to your external appearance is not only an affront to a holy God—who has called you to be the best you can be in order to glorify him—but also a failure to love your husband in a complete and caring way.

In what way are you exempt from needing marriage counseling if you have been careless to the needs of your husband? In what way have you been unaware and/or unconcerned about the visual desires and expectations your husband has? In what way are you greater than the need for a different perspective on the pain you have been causing him, by not making your outward appearance more important to you in order to assist him in his sexual needs? Are you not dishonoring your God and your husband in an unbiblical fashion by showing no care to these specific needs of your husband? This is a hard pill to swallow, and I by no means offer it to you lightly. However, it has long been necessary for Christian women to take charge of their responsibilities before their husbands and more importantly, before God.

CHAPTER 10

Our Sacred Vows

By now, I pray that you are beginning to understand the important role that external beauty plays in your responsibility before God. In addition, I pray that God is doing some serious work in your heart and that you are beginning to understand your need to show care and love to your husband through what you do with your external appearance.

Keeping Your Vows

I will never forget June 5, 2010. That day I walked down the aisle to meet the man of my dreams, to take his last name, to vow to cherish and love him, and to leave that church as the legally married couple: Adam and Ashley Bowman. I cannot think about that day with less than a smile on my face. However, I not only have to smile as I think of the joy of that day in the ceremony, but I also smile as I realize how naïve each of us was to the full vow we were making before God to each other. It has been a great five years of marriage. I can honestly say I love my husband now more than I did the day I made that lifelong commitment to him. I can say that because I have been offered many opportunities to grow in love, to understand what it truly means, and to know what our vows truly represent before God.

Yes, on that day, we understood this was a lifelong commitment. Yes, we acknowledged (as much as any single person can) the roles we were taking on as husband and wife. Yes, we even knew our marriage was supposed to be an earthly picture of a spiritual truth. However, what we did not understand 100% was how much selflessness it would take to fulfill those vows and honor the Lord with the decisions we made individually and as a couple. I am sure we are not the only couple that looks fondly on the day we made our vows and also realizes the gravity of the decision made on that day. I challenge you to take a look back at what took place on that day and how it does or should influence what we do with our vow today.

As we look through the Scripture, we find numerous passages that address the making of vows. In the 21st Century, we might view a vow as simply a declaration of intent. But Scripture brings to light that God views covenant-making as sacred and the breaking of such a vow a sin. Ecclesiastes 5:4–6 says, "When you vow a vow to God, do not delay paying it, for he has no pleasure in fools. Pay what you vow. It is better that you should not vow than that you should vow and not pay. Let not your mouth lead you into sin, and do not say before the messenger that it was a mistake. Why should God be angry at your voice and destroy the work of your hands?" Here, it is obvious that God views vows as commitments that are meant to be kept and the breaking of a vow is cause for God's anger and justice. In fact, God calls the breaker of that vow "a fool." Deuteronomy 23:21–23 confirms this same statement, as does Numbers 30:2 and Leviticus 5:4–13.

Hebrews 6:18 reminds us that God's character does not allow for him to lie, to break a vow, or to change. Therefore, as his representatives on earth, we are called to the same level of faithfulness in keeping our word. You've made a vow to your husband. Perhaps you made the traditional wedding vow, which reads something like this: "I, (name), take you (name), to be my (wife/husband), to have and to hold from this day forward, for better or for worse, for richer, for poorer, in sickness and in health, to love and to cherish; from this day forward until death do us part."[54] Perhaps your vow looked and sounded a little different than this classic vow. Either way, I am willing to make the assumption that in your vow, you made the promise to love this man above all others. In that vow, you made the promise to love and cherish him, to offer yourself to him, and to not allow anything to divide you except death.

So, where does physical attraction fall into this vow? How does external beauty line up with what you vowed to your husband that day so many or so few years ago? When you vowed to love him, you vowed to hold to the definition of love, which includes the description "it does not insist on its own way."[55] That is also the definition of humility according to Philippians 2.[56] In short, you have vowed to walk in humility with the man that you love. By making a vow to this man, you make a covenant promising to love your husband, to not seek your own, and to count his needs as greater than your own. His needs. That includes his sexual needs. That includes what is important to him versus what you might view as a priority. That includes the external, the visual, and the physically attractive.

If you would think this understanding is a stretch, I welcome you to take a look at the direct marriage-related commands stated in 1 Corinthians 7. Paul calls married couples to physical, sexual service to one another, specifically challenging the married

---

[54] http://weddings.about.com/od/weddingvows/a/traditionalvows.htm
[55] 1 Corinthians 13:5
[56] According to Philippians 2:3–5, humility looks like this: "Do nothing from selfish ambition or conceit, but in humility count others more significant than yourselves. Let each of you look not only to his own interests, but also to the interests of others. Have this mind among yourselves, which is yours in Christ Jesus."

woman to realize that her body is not her own. It belongs to her husband. "For the wife does not have authority over her own body, but the husband does."[57] Of course this is a two-way street as the second half of the verse continues: "Likewise the husband does not have authority over his own body, but the wife does."[58]

So, married woman, as you think about your marriage vows, understand that the covenant you have made to love and serve your husband is not limited. It is not a commitment only to serve him in the kitchen, or to faithfully to "stay together" through thick and thin, through sickness and health, through happy times and sad times. Its reach extends to the giving of yourself to him, wholly and physically. Taking care of your externals and making sure you are as healthy, fit, and physically attractive to your man is a specific way that you can fulfill that vow. Make yourself physically attractive to him for the purpose of honoring him, keeping your vows, and assisting him by meeting his God-designed needs. Experience being blessed by the Lord as you give yourself wholly to the man you have vowed to love and serve, not because he promises a husband who will always respond the way he should, but because God is a rewarder of those who follow through with their vows.[59]

Inspired to make some changes yet? If you are beginning to understand your responsibility before God and your husband but are not yet convinced, I would like to show you what life looks like for a man in this sex-selling society. After all, you can only meet his needs as completely as you are willing to know and understand this man that you have vowed to love. In order to do this effectively, we must learn what needs men have as a whole, what struggles they experience daily, and what is the best way to help your man specifically. So, before we look in detail at your

---

[57]   1 Corinthians 7:4a

[58]   1 Corinthians 7:4b

[59]   Hebrews 11:6

responsibility to assist your husband in keeping his vows, let's take a closer look at your husband and what we often forget is God-designed: his sexuality.

His God-Created Design

In a world where sex has become commercialized and pornography is always at one's fingertips, the understanding of men's interest and desire for sex has been twisted. So much so that we find ourselves seeing the male species' sexuality as somehow inherently sinful. There is obvious cause for concern, when we understand the deception of sin in our own lives and the temptation to twist our natural desires into something self-serving. But we also need to take a step back and understand something extremely important: God created your husband as a sexual being.

Genesis 2 and the creation of mankind are quickly found to involve sexuality. Verse 20 of chapter 2 discusses the fact that after naming all the animals, "for Adam there was not found a helper fit for him." God finds it necessary that Adam have a companion who matches his needs. While women would be tempted to define these "needs" as emotional or relational needs, another verse quickly follows challenging that with the clear introduction of sexual intercourse: "Therefore a man shall leave his father and his mother and hold fast to his wife, and they shall become one flesh. And the man and his wife were both naked and were not ashamed."[60] Only 55 verses into the first book of the Bible, God has already introduced the concept of man's sexual needs and the beauty of a united sexual relationship in marriage. He has created a pair that is "fit" for each other, that "become one flesh" and who

---

[60] Genesis 2:24–25

are then told immediately following creation to "be fruitful and multiply." Sex is God-created, God-designed, beautiful, and holy.

With that understood, we then have to see that man's interest in sex, his high sex drive, and his interest in the beauty and body of the womanly species is all God-designed. It is not a mistake. We can understand that concept. After all, we too are sexual beings. However, men's sexuality is hardly the same as women's. Our sexual feelings are often a response to emotional feelings. Men, on the other hand, operate much differently. Sometimes "different" can make us wonder if something is natural or designed as God would have it.

God is the ultimate designer and the divine creator, and nothing he has designed is a mistake. Psalm 139:13–15 reads: "For you formed my inward parts; you knitted me together in my mother's womb. I praise you, for I am fearfully and wonderfully made. Wonderful are your works; my soul knows it very well. My frame was not hidden from you, when I was being made in secret, intricately woven in the depths of the earth. Your eyes saw my unformed substance; in your book were written, every one of them, the days that were formed for me, when as yet there was none of them." More specifically, God did not design men and women to respond to sexual stimuli the same way. There have been a variety of studies done over a number of years that journal the physical and mental response differences between men and women.[61] Each study used visual stimuli to research and record arousal in the brain and body of both male and female subjects. While women and men both responded physically to the visual stimulation in these studies, there was a significant difference in the amount of arousal in a man's body versus a woman's body.

---

[61] http://www.theblaze.com/stories/2013/12/02/the-difference-between-men-and-womens-brains-revealed-in-this-photo/; http://www.sciencedaily.com/releases/2013/12/131202161935.htm; http://www.webmd.com/balance/features/how-male-female-brains-differ

Visual stimulation consisting merely of physical appearance that did not include the emotional appeals of a story line or relationship aroused men over two times more than it aroused women. In fact, whole areas of the brain were activated in men that remained unaffected for women. On the other hand, women proved to be more aroused by relationship development and appeals to the emotional as well as the physical.

Other studies have shown that the brain of a male subject fires transmissions upon the sight of a beautiful woman that offers the same kind of release and pleasure that drugs (specifically cocaine) and alcohol would offer synthetically. It has been scientifically proven that cocaine offers the user a feeling of self-confidence, energy, euphoria, and an overall freedom from normal social anxieties[62]. While a drug is not God-intended and divinely designed, it is useful to understand the kind of physical and mental release and addictive quality involved with a man and the arousal brought on by visual stimulation.

Additional research demonstrates other radical findings that reveal that when men reviewed a picture of a scantily clad woman for less than half a second, the memory recalled was that of a body without a head. In fact, areas of the brain that are utilized in consideration of another person as a relational being were not even activated. The area of the brain activated during the viewing of bikini-clad women was the same area of the brain utilized when the men considered something a "tool—something to use for one's own gain. The more suggestive the visual stimuli, the less the relational potential area of the brain was activated, and the more the objectification of the stimulant was made known.[63]

---

[62] http://addictions.about.com/od/cocaine/a/What-Do-Cocaine-Effects-Feel-Like.htm; http://www.ncbi.nlm.nih.gov/pmc/articles/PMC181074/

[63] http://m.neogaf.com/showthread.php?t=550060; http://www.mitpressjournals.org/doi/abs/10.1162/jocn.2010.21497; http://www.dailyprincetonian.com/2009/02/17/22773/; http://www.scientific

While our first reaction is to be disgusted by the way the male brain works, let us take an emotional step back. It is not a mistake that a man responds the way he does to visual stimulation. We see nothing in the Scripture about this being an effect of the fall of man and the introduction of sin. No, this is God-created! This is God-intended. This is a part of God's perfect design. It does not take much research to understand that God has designed the male gender very differently sexually than the female gender. However, knowing this fact can be life altering and revolutionary as you learn to meet your husband's sexual needs. More specifically, it is my prayer that this perspective of God's design not only humbles us at the amazing creator we serve but also inspires us to learn this new language of the male mind and how to be a biblical "help meet" in a way that matches the original plan of creation.

Simply put, your man is a visual creature. His mind and body react to what he sees and your responsibility to him involves meeting the specific needs that he has—needs that might not look anything like yours and desires that might not look anything like yours. However, that difference does not excuse your responsibility to meet those needs and fulfill your role as his wife. No, in fact, let these clear differences inspire you to make needed changes in your life in regards to what you are offering your husband as visual stimulation.

Helping Him Keep His Vows

It is not an easy task it understand how your vow to your husband includes giving him your best with your externals as a practical expression of putting his needs above yours. It is selfless,

---

american.com/article.cfm?id=how-our-brains-turn-women-into-objects; http://news.nationalgeographic.com/news/2009/02/090216-bikinis-women-men-objects.html; http://www.theguardian.com/science/2009/feb/16/sex-object-photograph

time-consuming, sacrificial, and humbling. However, there are great rewards for obedience to God and what he has called you to. God has called you as a married woman to be a "help meet" and in the most practical sense, that job description entails helping him fulfill his responsibilities before the Lord. Setting aside physical needs from the equation, his responsibility is to fulfill his God-given purpose as a member of mankind.

As creatures designed by creator God, our whole purpose as his creation is to bring God glory. Secondly, as a married man, your husband has an even harder task to fulfill. His eternal responsibility within earthly marriage is to act as a representation of the marriage union/complete unity of Christ and his Church. If you think for a moment that responding to a sinful man as the Church would respond to a holy God is hard, realize his responsibility calls for him to respond to a sinful wife with the love, selflessness, and patience that holy God has with his ever-failing church.

Do not get me wrong: you are not responsible for your husband's faithfulness to fulfill his own responsibilities. Nothing you do to assist him will remove from him a personal need to honor God with his life individually. That is something for which he is solely responsible. *Please also note*: I am not calling you to be your husband's personal Holy Spirit. No, as his help meet, you are called to assist him in any biblically supportable way to help him fulfill this duty. One way to do that practically is through your attention to external beauty.

Help him keep his vows! You are not responsible for his slip-up's, his giving in to temptation, and his lack of faithfulness to you in the way that God has called him to be. However you can assist your husband in throwing aside the temptations he faces in this world by caring about what is important to him. He will be tempted to give in to sexual lust, to click that suggestive news article, to watch that movie with "just one scene," and to take a second look at that billboard, magazine cover, or woman who walked by indecently dressed. These are real struggles he faces. You cannot bridle his eyes, his fingers, and his heart, but you can offer him something beautiful, physically attractive, sexually satisfying, and holy and honoring unto God! Failure to offer him a holy alternative does not give license to his struggle or justification for his sin, but it does show a lack of care for what you can control, as well as a lack of genuine love and concern for his soul before God and his needs before you.

There are so many arguments and justifications we make within our sinful, self-serving hearts, defending why we should not be forced to make sacrifices for someone else's growth. However, Paul himself challenges his fellow believers in Romans 14 and again in 1 Corinthians 10:24–33, to be willing to make personal sacrifices in order to assist others and guard them from sin: "Let no one seek his own good, but the good of his neighbor. Eat whatever is sold in the meat market without raising any question on the ground of conscience. For 'the earth is the Lord's, and the fullness thereof.' If one of the unbelievers invites you to dinner and you are disposed to go, eat whatever is set before you without raising any question on the ground of conscience. But if someone says to you, 'This has been offered in sacrifice,' then do not eat it, for the sake of the one who informed you, and for the sake of conscience—I do not mean your conscience, but his. For why should my liberty be determined by someone else's conscience? If I partake with thankfulness, why am I denounced because of that for which I give thanks? So, whether you eat or drink, or whatever you do, do all to the glory of God. Give no offense to Jews or to Greeks or to the church of God, just as I try to please everyone in everything I do, not seeking my own advantage, but that of many, that they may be saved."[64]

In this example, Paul is willing to forgo something as simple as meat sacrificed to a carved piece of wood for the good, the

---

[64]   1 Corinthians 10:24–31

conscience, and the growth of another. He declares that personal sacrifice is worth any personal loss for the sake of another's sanctification. How much more time, energy, and sacrifice to focus on being healthy and physically attractive be given to assist the man you vowed to love and serve in keeping his vow? The result is a couple who represents the beautiful relationship between Christ and the Church.

CHAPTER 11

Boundaries

Regardless of gender, before God, we are called to love and serve each other. We are called to walk in humility, preferring others and leaving no room for our fleshly hearts to view ourselves and our individual needs as more important than those of another. However, that leaves us vulnerable: vulnerable to being taken advantage of, to being treated poorly, and to being sinned against. After all, despite our focus to walk in the humility and love that was demonstrated by Christ for his people, we are still interacting with people who do not share that same purposeful mindset. Even if they desire to honor Christ like we do, they will eventually let us down, act selfishly, and fail to represent Christ to us in a complete manner. Take notice: you will let others down in the same ways.

Our intentions regarding the external strike close to home in our minds and hearts as fallen creatures. We quickly compare ourselves and set unreachable standards. In turn we judge and criticize others according to our own measure. Unfortunately, as sin has affected our hearts, so it has affected our ability to rightly communicate. Specifically, as women, it has damaged our ability to rightfully differentiate what is emotional, personal, or convicting from what is wrong before God.

When It's Not Ok to Say No

Perhaps you have found yourself defensive before others and before your spouse in this area. Your husband has challenged you, encouraged you, hinted to you, or even spoken outright regarding his interest in you focusing on becoming more physically attractive. Perhaps jokes have been made about your weight, your lack of physical fitness, or how different you are now than you were on your wedding day. Those jokes may bring external chuckles, but I know from personal experience that every joke brings with it internal pain. That pain, that ill treatment, that injustice, while painful and wrong, is not justification for you not doing your part to care about and give attention to what is eternally important— which includes what you do with your external appearance for the glory of God.

Therefore, guard your heart, my friend, from where the flesh would find justification for holding back. Perhaps it is time to address those past hurts with those who have caused self-conscious pain. Perhaps it is time to let go of the past situations in which you were made to feel inept, less than beautiful, or broken. Perhaps it is time to stop allowing those comments, jokes, and insults to control you and hold you back from your calling as a daughter of the King. After all, you are his prized, most-delicate creation. Perhaps it is time to move on from apathy and start giving your all to the man you have vowed to love with everything until your dying day. Whichever you situation, whatever your past, it is my prayer that you realize first your responsibility as a steward of God's perfect creation to do what you must. You might need to take hard steps and make necessary changes in order to bring the most glory to holy God with what he has given you—your body.

As a married woman, there are often times when we are tempted to say "no." I am not talking solely about sexual refusal here. Yes, that can be an issue with our gender, when selfishness, laziness, or self-consciousness holds us back from honoring God by offering ourselves sexually to our husband. However, I challenge you to start offering God your best by offering your husband your best, not only in the bedroom, but also in the kitchen, in the living room, and throughout all of life, as you offer him the best version of who you are, internally and externally. Do not let your past hold you back from the present and future. You are responsible for your part in your marriage relationship. You are responsible before God for maintaining a faithful representation of the heavenly marriage itself. Neither your past, your pain, nor your partner are justified, biblical excuses to say "no."

When It's Ok to Say No

Are there ever times to say "no" to your husband's desire for you to emphasize caring for your externals? Is there ever cause for stepping back and letting go of the image you have of what you should be externally? Yes, there are times and reasons for saying "no."

First and foremost, as a child of the King, the only justification for saying "no" is if the priorities you have in your life have become imbalanced. There is a problem if you're focusing more on the external and less on developing your internal beauty by resting in Christ. While these two are by no means mutually exclusive, prioritization in your life must be rooted in a desire to honor Christ. If your motives and actions have shifted so that his glory is not your number one goal with your externals, re-evaluation needs to take place.

As a married woman, the only biblical justification for withholding your body from your husband sexually is found in 1 Corinthians 7:5. It is acceptable when there is an understood and agreed upon season, after which time, coming together is a necessity: "Do not deprive one another, except perhaps by agreement for a limited time, that you may devote yourselves to prayer; but then come together again, so that Satan may not tempt you because of your lack of self-control." On a non-sexual level, the only biblically supportable reason for holding back from offering to your husband something that is visually attractive to him is if what he desires is sinful.

Please note: I am not talking about finding justification for not allowing what makes you uncomfortable or what takes you away from your safe concept of beauty. Remember, your body is not your own. The only situation I am discussing here is when your husband would rather you appear unhealthy (encouraging eating disorders, self-mutilation, etc.,) or would ask you to do something that is clearly stated as sin within the pages of Scripture. Those, my friend, are the only legitimate excuses for saying "no" when it comes to offering your everything to the man to whom you have vowed your faithfulness and love.

Is this a broad statement to make about a personal topic? Yes. Is this something that I have fully mastered in my own life? No. However, know that as a fellow sister in Christ and married woman, I too seek to honor God with all that I am—my externals included—and to be the wife that God calls me to biblically. Join me as we make the necessary steps to bring God glory with our external bodies.

CONCLUSION

Now What?

A book like this can be overwhelming. So much has been offered in an area where our flesh can so easily rise up and seek to justify what we have or have not been doing. Whether there has been wrong motivation or rationalization of valid pain, a rough past, personal and health issues, or anything else the devil or our flesh might find to keep us handcuffed to a weight that encumbers our ability to bring glory to God. In the words of Paul, "let us run with endurance the race that is set before us, looking to Jesus, the founder and perfecter of our faith, who for the joy that was set before him endured the cross, despising the shame, and is seated at the right hand of the throne of God."[65]

Now what? What do you need to throw aside in order to run this race in the most effective and God-honoring way possible? What do you need to let go of in order to move from a place of self-pity or bitterness or self-deprecation? What do you need to do to turn from what you have been viewing as useless, painful, or too personal in order to finally bring glory to God in this area of your life?

No, this is not a 12-step program with my personal plan for

---

[65] Hebrews 12:1–2

physical perfection attained by the final week. No, this is not my workout plan imposed on your life with claims of results you will or won't see. This is not promises guaranteed regarding how your life, marriage, and health will be revolutionized forever. This is my appeal to you to take the truth about the importance of the externals and apply these principles to your life in the way that God is challenging you to act.

Perhaps your journey needs to start with a few hard conversations with your family, your spouse, or your pastor about what you have found to be sin issues in your life—sin because you've held back from giving your all to Christ and to your spouse if you're married. Perhaps it is time to care, to eat healthier, to talk to your doctor, to set up an exercise regimen, to start taking walks, or to be disciplined, self-controlled, and God-glorifying in what you eat, drink, and do. Perhaps it is time to re-evaluate your motives. Perhaps you have done all the "right" things, but you've been motivated by a self-seeking heart, creating a standard that has been set in your own mind and which is never quite met. Perhaps you have forgotten that you are called to do it all "to the glory of God."[66]

God is calling you to make changes in your life, my friends. My sisters, I ask you to evaluate where you are in your stewardship of your physical body and to pray for wisdom on how to apply the truth that God has revealed to you.

> James 1:22–25 "But be doers of the word, and not hearers only, deceiving yourselves. For if anyone is a hearer of the word and not a doer, he is like a man who looks intently at his natural face in a mirror. For he looks at himself and goes away and at once forgets what he was like. But the one who looks into the perfect law, the law of liberty, and perseveres, being no hearer who forgets but a doer who acts, he will be blessed in his doing."

---

[66] 1 Corinthians 10:31

Printed in the United States
By Bookmasters